LOVE
HEALS
PRACTICE GUIDE

LOVE
HEALS
PRACTICE GUIDE

A 21-DAY JOURNEY
TO PERSONAL TRANSFORMATION

ILCHI LEE AND
ILCHIBUKO TODD

BEST
LIFE
MEDIA

952 E. Baseline Rd., Suite 101
Gilbert, AZ 85204
www.BestLifeMedia.com
480-926-2480

First paperback edition: July 2024
Library of Congress Control Number: 2024937347
ISBN-13: 978-1-947502-29-1

Cover and interior design by Kiryl Lysenka

To all who brave the journey of self-love.

CONTENTS

INTRODUCTION
By Ilchi Lee

"Can I dash down to the first floor and come right back up?" Bumwoon asked, his eyes lit with a spark of anticipation. "Absolutely," I replied, but he was already bounding toward the stairs. Moments later, he returned, slightly out of breath but with a wide, triumphant smile. "I just ran up three flights of stairs without stopping!"

Just a couple of hours earlier, climbing to the third floor of our building, which had no elevator, was a significant challenge for him. He had to pause multiple times to catch his breath. Bumwoon, a dedicated Korean-American entrepreneur from Philadelphia, had been battling with chronic fatigue ever since he lost one of his kidneys to failure.

Mornings were particularly tough; he would wake up feeling like his body was made of lead. Simple tasks exhausted him, and he often skipped evening routines to collapse into bed. Despite following his doctor's advice on medications, diet, and exercise, his condition barely improved. For someone once nicknamed "Iron Man" for his relentless energy, accepting this new, draining lifestyle was nothing short of a nightmare. The thought of having to live with extreme fatigue and weakness forever terrified him.

During a visit to South Korea, he sought me out after reading about my work with energy practices, hoping for a turnaround. My evaluation revealed considerable energy blockages in his body. I encouraged him to tap into and activate his inner energy during guided sessions. To his astonishment, his body started moving spontaneously at some point—twisting, stretching, shaking—without any conscious effort from him. "My body's moving all by itself," he marveled, surprised at how effortless it felt. "Exactly," I affirmed. "You're doing wonderfully. This is your body's way of liberating itself from blockages, circulating energy where it's needed most. Your body is healing itself. Trust in this process." Having fully engaged, Bumwoon ended his session drenched in sweat but invigorated.

He was amazed at how light his body felt, so he ran back down and up the stairs to check it out for himself. "What did you do to me?" he asked. I explained, "I just guided you. Your body's natural healing and energy took care of the rest. You've tapped into your own healing power."

Encouraged by the notable change from day one, Bumwoon wholeheartedly took to the practices I taught him, making them a part of his everyday life. Each day of his stay in South Korea brought him noticeable health benefits. "It's like I'm waking up from a long slumber," he'd say, feeling more alive and energized every morning—a joy he thought was gone for good. Back in the U.S., he wrote me a sincere letter about his journey to feeling better and his newfound wish to help others heal.

"I was so wrapped up in growing my business that I hardly noticed the world around me. But after becoming seriously ill and then regaining my health, I began to see my life differently. I realized the value of each moment and am now committed to living a more meaningful life. Experiencing self-healing through your guidance was a revelation for me, and I want to help others discover this path to wellness. I'm organizing a group of people; would you come and share your practices with us?"

His words inspired me to travel to the U.S. to give public talks and host workshops, a first in the country. This initiative led to the opening of the first training center in 1991, where we introduced Korea's ancient energy principles and practices to a new audience.

As I have found in my work with many people, Bumwoon's story tells an important truth: we all have the power to heal ourselves, and we have the power to start a ripple effect of healing far beyond our immediate reach. This journey of discovery and healing is at the heart of my life's work, and it is the essence of this book.

How the *Love Heals* Film Was Made

During the COVID-19 pandemic, the widespread anxiety, fear, and helplessness people felt deeply concerned me. I wanted to transform these feelings into hope and faith for a brighter future. Motivated by this goal, I decided to create a new film to make self-care and healing accessible to everyone, helping them take charge of their mental and physical health.

While seeking creative collaborators for my film project, I met Krisanna and Dana, two individuals deeply committed to personal development and spirituality. Krisanna was actively searching for ways to aid Dana, who was grappling with chronic pain and exploring various healing models. United by our shared vision of fostering a kinder, more mindful world, we instantly connected. Krisanna, as a director and videographer, began to document Dana's healing journey, marking the start of our collaborative venture.

The film production team hosted a retreat in Sedona, Arizona, to explore the healing potential of energy practice on individuals struggling with physical and emotional pain. For four nights and five days, 18 participants joined the film crew on an exploration of healing. The stories and journeys of these individuals became the highlight of the film *Love Heals*, with Dana's story at its heart. Since its release in 2022, it has reached and inspired millions, demonstrating the power of self-healing and offering hope to many.

About the *Love Heals Practice Guide*

The book you're reading serves as a companion to the *Love Heals* film, deepening its insights and their practical use. Ilchibuko, the lead trainer at the retreat showcased in the film, guided the participants through their journeys. Now, she shares the essence of the method featured in the film, showing how you, too, can start your journey of self-discovery and healing.

Ilchibuko is an exceptional teacher, deeply versed in energy principles and practices. Her dedication to helping others and her talent and experience enable her to share these teachings effectively. During more than 20 years of teaching, she has helped thousands access their greatest potential.

As the former president and program director of the Sedona Mago Center for Well-being and Retreat, Ilchibuko has led many retreats and workshops. These events, focusing on self-discovery, self-healing, and spirituality, have attracted participants from around the world. Currently, as CEO of Body & Brain Yoga, she collaborates with instructors at 80 centers across the U.S., focusing on enhancing health and wellness for individuals and communities.

This book radiates Ilchibuko's heartfelt dedication and commitment to your healing and personal growth journey. Her authenticity lights the way, steering you toward the profound truths, deep love, and remarkable healing abilities within you.

The *Love Heals Practice Guide* lets you harness the incredible potential within yourself for both physical and emotional well-being. In this book, you will explore universal principles of energy and discover how to apply them to heal your body and mind. At the core of this path to healing is the practice of self-love, an indispensable element of your personal growth. With self-love at its foundation, this guide invites you to unlock a world where healing and growth can flourish.

By exploring and experiencing energy through practices like those in this book, I met my true self. I realized that I am life itself—infinite, immeasurable, complete, and beautiful. I was so moved that I fell in love with myself. This experience also showed me that the great life energy I felt is my essence and the essence of all people and things in the universe. I believe that when we recognize and embody the absolute value of our true selves, we can change our individual lives and the world as a whole.

There is no greater joy or inspiration for me than seeing individuals realize their potential to effect change in their lives and the world. The *Love Heals* film and this book were created to remind people of the great potential within each of us. The love and creativity we all possess can heal individual and global pain, bridge divisions, and create a new and better future for our planet.

Together with Ilchibuko, Krisanna, Dana, and everyone involved in the *Love Heals* film, I hope both the film and this book will direct you toward the life you aspire to live. I also hope the messages contained in this book contribute to making our world and the Earth a more mindful and peaceful place. The energy principles and practices you're about to explore have helped millions achieve true healing and consciously shape their lives. Now, it's your turn to start that journey.

SPECIAL INTRODUCTION
By Dana Croschere

Reflecting on the journey of creating *Love Heals*, I am overwhelmed with gratitude. This film gave purpose to my pain. For years, I felt like a victim, struggling to get out of bed each day, feeling robbed of a *normal life*.

I couldn't understand how my life shifted from an extremely active lifestyle to experiencing debilitating discomfort. I certainly had no idea how much my trapped emotions, trauma, a dysregulated nervous system, and the inability to accept and love myself contributed to my suffering.

I continued to hope for the day I would be pain-free, but the longer I suffered, the more defeated I felt. I could have never predicted how much this pain journey would become the greatest catalyst for transformation in my life.

If you've watched *Love Heals*, you know my story is woven throughout the fabric of the film. My ongoing struggle with chronic pain and two unsuccessful spine surgeries ultimately led me to connect with the most authentic part of myself—what I call my true self. This connection forever changed my life.

I owe this transformation in part to Ilchibuko, who guided me through powerful ancient practices toward connecting with my true self. I am forever grateful to her for her heartfelt dedication to helping those like me. This deep connection led me to stop drinking alcohol and then awakened a part of me that was ready to live out my purpose, giving me the strength to leave a corporate job and pursue the life of my dreams.

It reminds me of the very beginning when Krisanna and I first met with Ilchi Lee to discuss creating a documentary about healing, and he shared with us the two most important messages he hoped the film would convey: the belief that you are your own best healer, and the importance of self-love.

When we first heard these words, we had no idea what the film would become or how it would all unfold, and we certainly would have never predicted the impact it would have.

Several years later, *Love Heals* has won multiple film festival awards, secured a national broadcast on PBS, is currently streaming on Gaia, and continues to be shared at in-person and virtual events worldwide in over 11 languages, touching literally millions of lives.

Some tell us they felt hope for the first time and have used the tools from our film to take tangible steps toward healing. This is all we could have asked for in creating *Love Heals,* and it makes everything I experienced during the darkest days of my healing journey worthwhile. So now, I say thank you to my pain—for it has helped me discover the greatest life I could have ever imagined.

If you are on a healing journey yourself, or perhaps you love someone who is, my prayer for you in watching *Love Heals* and reading this guide is that you feel hope. Hope gave me the strength I needed to get to where I am today, and I pray you will find it for yourself, too.

Above all else, always remember: you are your own best healer, and the journey of loving yourself is the greatest journey you will ever take.

LETTER TO THE READERS
By Ilchibuko Todd

Dear friends,

Being part of the *Love Heals* film was an unforgettable experience in my life. Having met numerous people through retreats, workshops, and conferences over two decades, the healing space we created together at the Love Heals Retreat stands out as truly remarkable.

In that transformative space, I witnessed a profound shift in many lives. Anna, who had been struggling with a debilitating heart condition, found the will to live once again. Chad, who had been holding on to anger toward his father for many years, could finally forgive him. Katriana, who had always felt anxious and unsettled, experienced a deep sense of peace and stability. And Leah, who had always felt like she didn't belong, finally was able to love and accept herself for who she was.

The 18 souls I encountered through the *Love Heals* film were nothing short of messengers; each one showed us the power and beauty of true healing. They taught us that within each of us lies an unbreakable love, a force strong enough to withstand the greatest of pains and transform it into healing and growth. To this day, each time I watch the touching stories of the retreat participants in the film, the emotions from that time resurface, often moving me to tears.

After the film's release, Krisanna, Dana, and I traveled across the U.S., showcasing *Love Heals* at various screenings, conferences, and retreats. During these events, a recurring question emerged from many attendees:

"How can I experience a similar healing journey?"

In response to this widespread interest, I've led the Love Heals Retreat in Sedona. To broaden the reach of these powerful experiences, I've decided to write a book with Ilchi Lee. This book aims to share the retreat's powerful insights and healing opportunities with a wider audience, making the essence of our Sedona retreats accessible to more people.

My mission is to inspire hope and equip you with the belief that you have the inner strength to overcome any difficulties and pain you face, and that you can achieve holistic health across physical, emotional, and mental dimensions. I aim to help *you* experience true healing, just like the individuals in the film and the millions of others who have transformed their lives using these energy principles and tools.

The Teachings Behind This Book

I've seen many people, including myself, experience significant healing and transformation through the ancient energy principles and practices modernized by Ilchi Lee. When I first embraced these practices, I was professionally established and successful but unhappy. Under Ilchi Lee's guidance, I embarked on a self-discovery journey, shedding my external identity and societal labels to find my true self. This path led to a life purpose that resonates deeply with my soul. Over the past 20 years of working with Ilchi Lee, I've been sharing the joy and fulfillment I've discovered, hoping to inspire similar transformations in the lives of others.

I am presenting this book in my voice to have a more direct, personal connection with you. However, this book's content is deeply rooted in the teachings and energy principles developed by Ilchi Lee. He is not just the source of inspiration but also the primary creator of the practices you're about to dive into.

Adapted from Korea's ancient mind-body practices, his methods are now known worldwide as Brain Education. They have impacted many lives, reaching beyond individuals to influence businesses, schools, and communities. Ilchi Lee's unwavering belief that we have the power to shape our destiny and influence the course of humanity has inspired countless people. His vision has also sparked various global projects and movements in education, sustainability, and charity.

How to Use This Book

This book is based on the essential principle that we're made up of energy and have a body, mind, and soul. When these three aspects of our being work together, real health and true happiness happen. When they're in sync, the magic of healing can begin. But what binds body, mind, and soul together? Energy. Energy is the force that has the power to bind these fundamental aspects of ourselves together. Consider this book your guide on a journey toward reconnecting your body, mind, and soul. By unlocking their combined potential, you can create the healing and life changes you seek.

The *Love Heals Practice Guide* carries a singular message applicable to any life challenge you may be facing, whether it's physical pain, emotional distress, or mental hurdles: *"Come home to yourself and find everything you need within you."*

By embracing this philosophy and returning to your true self, you will experience true healing. The energy principles and practices detailed in this book are your guides on this journey. They offer a pathway back to your true self, unlocking the potential for deep healing and personal fulfillment within you.

This book is divided into two parts to assist you on your path to healing.

In Part 1: The Healing Process, you'll explore the essential energy principles that are key to healing, as seen in the retreat highlighted in the film. It shares real stories from people who have experienced remarkable healing using these principles, alongside insights from experts in the field. This section aims to deepen your understanding of how these energy principles can actively support your healing journey.

Part 2: The 21-Day Journey guides you through specific training and meditation techniques that bring the energy principles to life over three weeks. These techniques are easy to follow, so everyone can try them, whether you're new to these practices or not. You'll learn how to connect deeply with your body, mind, and soul, leading to a greater sense of love.

To enhance your experience with some exercises, I've included QR codes that link to YouTube videos. These videos provide visual demonstrations to help you perform the exercises more easily and effectively.

As you dive into the pages of this book, you will find that we often revisit certain ideas. And trust me, there's a good reason for it. To truly master these energy principles and let them become ingrained, we must address them repeatedly. Think of each repetition as another layer of understanding, another step closer to your healing.

I hope this book instills deep hope and unwavering belief in your healing power. As we begin, I encourage you to open your mind and heart to the transformative power you hold within and find your own story of healing and self-discovery.

PART 1

THE
HEALING
PROCESS

CHAPTER 1

COMING HOME
TO YOURSELF

"What has brought you here?" This is the first question I often ask those who join us at the Love Heals Retreat. The retreats attract people from all walks of life—locals from the Sedona area, visitors from all over the United States and Canada, and others from different countries around the world. When individuals commit time and money to a five-day retreat, I know they expect something substantial.

Dana, a central figure in the *Love Heals* film, was one of those seekers. In 2017, Dana's life took an unexpected turn when she injured a calf muscle while jogging on a treadmill. Initially, the pain was manageable, but it soon spread to her upper legs, her sciatic nerve, and eventually her back. Dana visited numerous doctors over the course of a year, yet none could identify the source of her pain. A diagnosis came only after an MRI revealed what was going on: the intense pain was caused by a herniated disc pressing on a nerve. Surgery was the recommended course of action.

After months of agonizing contemplation, Dana finally opted for surgery when the pain made even walking a struggle. Yet, a few weeks post-surgery, she made a terrifying discovery—her spinal fluid was leaking, and she needed a second surgery. Lying in the ICU, the pain was so relentless that she found herself begging for relief. Even after the surgery, Dana's pain continued to intensify, leaving her devastated. What was meant to alleviate her suffering seemed to be making it worse.

Before her surgery, Dana had sought relief from her chronic pain through various avenues—alternative treatments, personal development workshops, and calming methods like yoga and meditation. She attended a workshop at Sedona Mago Center, where she discovered energy training and connected with her true self for the first time. This experience planted a seed that sparked a chain of events, leading her to share her story and experience the retreat depicted in the *Love Heals* film.

Many individuals I encounter at the retreats share similar stories. They come in search of solutions for their physical and emotional suffering, often battling chronic illnesses and emotional traumas. Despite prior attempts at conventional treatments, such as surgery, medication, and counseling, they've found no respite. So, they arrive at the retreat with a glimmer of hope, looking for an alternative path to healing.

People also come to the retreat when they're going through major life changes or searching for a new path in life. These transitions can be emotionally challenging, like going through a painful divorce or grieving the loss of a loved one. Others might be at a crossroads, thinking about changing their life's direction entirely.

Take Kris, for instance. He has been married for 17 years, and it has been anything but a harmonious union. His marriage lacks love, emotional stability, shared interests, and mutual respect. Arguments and disputes have been the norm in their relationship, escalating to the point where both have exploded in anger and said deeply hurtful things to the other. Divorce had been suggested a few years ago, but Kris was determined to shield his children from the pain he felt during his parents' divorce when he was 12. He decided to choose his children over divorce, no matter how dire things became.

Today, Kris and his wife barely speak to each other and sleep in separate rooms. Family meals have devolved into moments of prolonged awkward silence, driving their children to make excuses and quickly leave the table. Kris now finds himself at a crossroads, questioning whether continuing this unhappy marriage is truly in the best interest of his children. He turned to the Love Heals Retreat, seeking clarity on the path forward.

Some people come to the retreat seeking a way out of feeling stuck in life. They are in a rut, like a car spinning its wheels in mud. They wake up to the same dull daily routine, feeling trapped and frustrated. They want to change, but it feels impossible, and they don't know where to begin. They're restless and want to break free from this feeling of being stuck and unfulfilled.

Nancy's story mirrors the experiences of many in this group. She feels like all the vibrancy has drained from her life, leaving her in a colorless world. Despite a decade-long career and a decent salary as a manager at an insurance company, she finds no joy in her work. Constantly watching the clock in the afternoons, she feels drained. Even returning home after work brings no relief. She spends evenings and weekends asleep, devoid of any desire for other activities. An overwhelming feeling of exhaustion, both physically and emotionally, has taken hold. She's reached a point where she wishes to disappear, and this thought terrifies her. At the urging of a friend, Nancy decided to travel to Sedona and join the retreat.

At some point in life, each of us experiences something akin to what Dana, Kris, and Nancy have been through. For various reasons, we find ourselves at low points or pivotal moments in life, wrestling with physical, mental, and emotional anguish, big and small. And in these moments, we yearn for a way out of that suffering.

If you're reading this book, you may be searching for something, too. You might feel lethargic and disconnected, yearning to rekindle your interest in people and the world around you. Perhaps you're battling persistently negative emotions and despair or dealing with a chronic illness. You may be grappling with the stress and anxiety of addictions, whether it's overeating, alcohol, gambling, drugs, or sex, and you're in pursuit of a way out. Despite having everything—money, a great job, and a wonderful family—you may feel an inner void, a lack of purpose and meaning. Everything might appear to be unraveling, and you have an urgent sense that this can't continue. Or maybe you picked up this book after watching the *Love Heals* film, or you're reading it to help someone you know.

No matter why you're reading this book, I truly appreciate your presence, which allows us to connect. Even if you're unsure about what you seek, there's a part of you that desires change and awakening. While you explore this book, I hope you discover the clarity you're seeking and that you find the path to a more meaningful life.

The Journey of Self-Discovery

I have made an important discovery through countless interactions with individuals attending various retreats and workshops, including Love Heals. When people meet their true selves, a deep transformation and significant healing unfold, irrespective of the issues or motivations that initially brought them here.

I've witnessed these moments time and time again. The reality of healing by reconnecting with one's true self is akin to a universal law. It is reliable, like the law of gravity or water boiling at 100 degrees Celsius. Usually, people find what they've been seeking within themselves, not somewhere in the external world. In that moment, a beautiful and powerful transformation takes place. Ultimately, every healing journey is about coming home to oneself.

Everyone desires health, happiness, and fulfillment. However, we often mistakenly believe that these treasures lie beyond our reach. We tirelessly pursue something or someplace in search of happiness, thinking that, once achieved, life will finally bestow joy and contentment upon us.

Reflect on your life for a moment. You've likely had numerous goals that you believed would bring you happiness. Some you've achieved, and others have remained elusive. When you've worked hard to attain a desired goal, there's a sense of accomplishment and happiness. But it seldom endures. Soon, something feels missing, leaving you unfulfilled. You may start to believe that what you truly desire is something else or somewhere else, and you set off in pursuit. You may strive to secure a more satisfying job, find a partner who loves you more, or create a cozier living environment. We often live our lives in this repetitive cycle.

In our relentless pursuit of external achievements that we hope will satisfy us, we eventually realize that true happiness isn't outside us; it resides within. While external circumstances and events can trigger these feelings, our ultimate desire is for inner richness and the lasting contentment only found in the depths of our hearts. These things cannot be found in the external world; they're experienced when we turn our attention inward.

Have you ever felt a deep sense of peace inside? These are moments when anxiety, impatience, and loneliness simply melt away. Have you ever found yourself in the darkness that seemed never-ending and all-encom-passing, only to watch it suddenly dissipate like lifting fog, exposing the way forward? Have you ever lost all motivation for life but then found a surge of passion for life emerging from within you? Have you ever been brought to tears when you realized you've always been surrounded by love, even if you felt it was missing before?

This is just a small part of what you experience when you return to your true self.

Returning to Your True Self

Many individuals who embark on journeys of self-healing hold a misconception: they believe they are broken, inadequate, or lacking, and they must fix themselves. They perceive their current self as flawed, falling short of their own expectations and of others, and they believe themselves undeserving of love. As a result, they feel the need to change their imperfections and escape the conditions, people, and situations that make them unhappy.

This misconception is far from the truth. We are not broken, inadequate, or lacking, because our true selves remain untouched by any harm, wounds, or damage. Within this understanding of the true self, there is no self-blame, no fear, no painful past, and no self-doubt. Our true selves are already perfect, whole, and complete.

You might wonder, "But when I look within, I don't see that completeness. I'm filled with self-blame, complaints, and pain." If that's how you feel, don't stop there. Dig deeper.

Who is the one watching yourself, the one noticing that you're blaming yourself, feeling dissatisfied, and enduring pain? Who recognizes that your current state falls short of your true desires? Who keeps you from giving up on the quest for happiness and peace? All of these questions point to one answer—your true self.

The "you" that you typically notice, the one burdened with feelings of inadequacy, brokenness, or disorientation, isn't your true self. This self is what we call the ego, the product of a lifetime shaped by societal expectations, family values, and the roles we play in our lives—a son, daughter, spouse, employee, and so forth. We've been told who we should be, how we should act, and what success looks like.

Through it all, we've internalized these external definitions and created a self-image based on how others see us. This self-image can leave us feeling perpetually unsatisfied, forever chasing material possessions, success, wealth, status, and other achievements as measures of our worth. The never-ending comparisons and competition with others lead to anxiety, worry, and fear. We feel we must outdo ourselves and everyone else, and when we fall short, we carry the belief that we are lacking and not good enough.

Some might have been fortunate to grow up in accepting and supportive environments, and others have risen above challenging circumstances. However, even their positive self-images are constructed. It's important to remember that you are not your name, your thoughts, your emotions, your achievements, or your failures. These are masks you wear, experiences your true self undergoes through your body and mind.

Your true nature transcends how others see you or how you see yourself. It remains untouched by whether your self-image is positive or negative. Your true self is whole and complete as it is, needing neither addition nor subtraction.

Reconnecting with your true self isn't about fixing feelings of inadequacy or unworthiness. It's not about becoming even more capable or attractive than you already are. It's about rediscovering the inherently complete self that has always existed beneath the constructed self you've come to know as "me."

Becoming your true self doesn't require achieving a specific goal or reaching a particular destination. Your true essence lacks nothing; it's already within you, here and now, desperately waiting for you to acknowledge and embrace it.

The Importance of Self-Connection

You might be wondering why connecting with your true self is so crucial. If you're generally content with your current life, you might think, "Why bother digging deeper?" There are many practical benefits to meeting your true self. When you come face-to-face with your true self, positive changes unfold in your life. Physical and emotional healing takes place, emotions are better regulated, insight and creativity soar, and your capacity to understand and embrace others deepens, fostering more fulfilling human connections.

But beyond these practical advantages, the most crucial reason to meet your true self is that it satisfies a deep inner need. At some point in life, most people must confront two fundamental questions: Who am I? What do I really want in life? We might not always articulate these questions in these exact words, but we all yearn to understand our identity and find purpose and direction that give our lives meaning.

Sometimes, even when everything seems fine on the surface, we feel an inner emptiness. It's like we have an unsolved puzzle, and we can't figure out what's missing. We might have success and good relationships, but there's still a lingering feeling that something isn't quite right. This feeling is often a longing for our true selves. This deep, continual feeling of loneliness and sadness can only be healed when we connect with our true selves. It's like finding the missing puzzle piece that makes us feel whole and complete.

If you don't know who you truly are, you also can't know what you truly want. When we're not in touch with our true selves, we miss the compass that helps us navigate life. We might chase after things that seem important, attractive, or impressive to others, but deep down, we lack that undeniable feeling that says, "This is my path."

Without a clear sense of what we truly want, we often become subject to fleeting thoughts, emotions, desires, and the expectations of others. It's like being carried by a strong current, but we're not sure where it's taking us. And when we lose touch with our true selves, we may prioritize things that don't align with what truly matters. We might conform to societal norms and other people's expectations, feeling out of sync with our true selves. This kind of existence can lead to a sense of emptiness and dissatisfaction, as if we're missing out on the actual experience of being alive.

Despite the countless individuals we encounter, the only constant presence from beginning to end is ourselves. So, the importance of meeting your true self goes beyond any other life experience or connection you'll ever encounter.

Reconnecting with your true self holds immense importance, even though the world may not always acknowledge it. Various obstacles can impede our journey back to our true selves. In addition to societal norms and conventions that tend to prioritize external and material values, our own thoughts, emotions, memories, and experiences often trick us into thinking that certain illusionary aspects of ourselves are true when, in fact, they are not.

Our day-to-day thoughts and emotions feel so real and tangible that we often confuse them for our true selves. Nevertheless, the truth is that our lives are essentially a spiritual journey toward our inner selves, even if they appear focused on external matters and the material world.

Many of life's problems and sufferings arise from not living in harmony with our true selves. So, when we do reconnect with our true selves, it brings us insight into resolving these problems. However, it's essential to understand that discovering your true self doesn't erase all your problems or make your suffering vanish as if by magic.

What truly changes is your perspective; you stop seeing yourself as lacking, broken, or empty. The self that once believed it was powerless to alter the situation no longer dominates. Connecting with your true self allows you to see your problems, suffering, and challenges from an entirely different angle.

As you encounter your true self, which is whole and complete, you discover an unparalleled deep comfort. You realize that your true self embodies infinite potential and unconditional love. This boundless love holds the power to dissolve the disappointments and hurts you've accumulated from the world, from others, and from yourself.

When you reunite with your true self, you can rise above life's daily conflicts, pains, and attachments. In this process, you uncover the precious being you are, wrapped in an indescribable sense of love. True healing begins with this love.

CHAPTER 2

BEING IN YOUR BODY

Knowing that every healing journey leads us back to ourselves, you may ask, "How can I reconnect with my true self?" The only way is through direct experience. While reading and hearing about the true self can deepen your understanding of the concept, that's not enough to truly encounter it. You can only meet your true self through firsthand experience.

People who have never been in love can't truly grasp what that feels like, no matter how much you try to explain it to them. But if you've ever loved someone deeply, you don't need anyone to describe what love feels like—you've already experienced it. Knowing your true self works in a similar way.

There are many ways to directly experience your true self. The spiritual and wisdom traditions of the world typically use methods like meditation, yoga, prayer, and contemplation of sacred texts. In this book, I will guide you to reconnect with your true self, starting with your body. Specifically, by awakening the body's senses, you tap into your body's inherent wisdom and pave the way to your true self.

Awakening the Body's Senses

How well do you know your body? How much do you care for it? Most of us focus a lot on our bodies, aiming for a slim, fit, muscular, or attractive appearance. Every day, the media bombards us with images of celebrities showing off these ideal bodies. A youthful, beautiful, and strong physique isn't just aesthetically pleasing anymore—it's become a symbol of social status. As a result, we invest a considerable amount of money, energy, and time toward achieving this ideal. It's almost like we're obsessed with creating the perfect body.

Many of us experience feelings of inferiority when comparing our bodies to these perceived ideals, thinking we might be too fat, too short, or not shaped right. This critical self-perception leads many to dislike or even hate their own bodies.

Although we take our bodies seriously and invest heavily in them, the truth is that most people are severely disconnected from their bodies because they are mainly interested in the "visible body." The visible body is the body that we can see and touch, the one that exists as an object on the physical plane. However, to experience genuine healing and connect with our true selves, it's essential to shift from "how others perceive my body" to "how my body feels to me."

Your body isn't just an image in others' minds or in yours. Height, weight, waist size, body mass index, blood pressure, blood sugar. . . these are measurements of your body's physical health and appearance, but they do not tell the whole story. Your body is a vibrant, living organism. Your body image or body indicators are evaluations of your body from the outside, but you can learn even more by going inside. You must "feel" your living body *from within*. Ask yourself, "How close am I to my body, and can I feel the life pulsing through me every second?" Awakening the senses in your body allows you to answer this question.

Anna's Story

Anna, from the *Love Heals* film, has a heart with a genetic condition that has always affected her life. Four years back, her heart got so weak that she needed surgery to get a pacemaker and defibrillator fitted. She starts her day every morning by checking her blood pressure and weight, logs these readings, and takes various medications. Because of complications from the pacemaker surgery, a follow-up surgery was needed, causing her to go several months without moving her left arm. Lack of movement caused a frozen shoulder, and after months of physical therapy, she had to go through yet another surgery.

Her heart condition leaves her feeling tired, so she often needs a daily nap. She takes multiple breaks during the day when she needs to perform routine activities, such as climbing the stairs. She can't even walk up the hill to get her mail without her husband by her side due to the risk of collapsing. Her doctor said that her next step would be to do a work-up for a heart transplant.

For the past four years, Anna's focus has been on her pacemaker and defibrillator because of her heart condition and the need to track her vital signs. She constantly monitors her heart rate, following her doctor's instructions on all the dos and don'ts for body movement, rest, medications, and limiting stress.

When she thinks about her body, she focuses on the cold metal in her heart and the numbers on the machines. Her heart felt like a dead space, a void because she was hyper-aware of the devices controlling it. She usually feels the lump of computerized metal weighing her down and the wires running from the computer to her heart muscle, forcing it to pump blood through her body.

After her experience at the Love Heals Retreat, she shared, "It might sound strange, but I felt that I have a body—my own body. I forgot I have a whole body that is here to serve me. This realization made me start with uncontrollable laughter and then massive tears because it was such an overwhelming feeling."

She deeply connected with her heart for the first time, experiencing a love beyond words unlike anything she had known before. Previously, thinking about her heart made her angry, bitter, resentful, and irritated. She was also scared, afraid her heart might stop at any moment. But now, Anna feels different. She exclaims, "I have this peace and comfort that I have a big, beautiful, amazing, loving heart. My body was telling me that it's okay to forget about the machines and let them work wonder-

fully for you. It's time to live with your beautiful heart."
She realized she had been taking her heart for granted,
forgetting to be thankful that it pushes life-giving blood
throughout her body.

Thinking about the Body vs. Feeling It

I've mentioned before that despite feeling broken, inadequate, or lost, the truth is that we are already whole.
Meeting our true selves isn't about fixing anything; it's
about returning to the essence of who we are, which is
already perfect as it is.

The same applies to our bodies. Many of us carry
negative feelings or thoughts of inadequacy about our
bodies, especially if we're dealing with chronic illness,
pain, or body image struggles. However, just like our true
selves, our bodies are already complete.

Certainly, some individuals are born with disabili-
ties, while others may lose some bodily functions from
accidents or illnesses. However, even with these challenges, our bodies remain perfect because they are an
integral part of our true selves, which are already whole
and complete. Awakening the body's senses isn't about
discovering entirely new sensations; it's about restoring
the inherent senses that our bodies naturally possess.
This process allows us to reconnect with the innate
wisdom and healing potential that resides within us.

One remarkable aspect of our bodies is their innate
ability to heal themselves, equipped with built-in

systems to sustain life. Maintaining health becomes effortless when we allow these systems to function without interference. This is because being healthy is life's most natural state. If our health is off track, our bodies try to get back to their natural balance. Medicines and surgeries aid in healing by turning down some of the body's reactions and boosting others. But it's really our body's inherent healing capacity that allows any treatment to work.

The intricate processes that support our bodies, including the remarkable phenomenon of natural healing, are truly amazing. Even if you're currently facing a serious illness or chronic pain, your body continues to breathe, your heart beats, and your blood flows without any conscious effort from you. This resilience is due to our body's inherent tendency and capability to return to balance and harmony. I believe that there is no such thing as a completely broken body. Regardless of the extent of the damage to it, the body maintains its innate capacity for healing, as bestowed by nature. By awakening our senses and tapping into our body's wisdom, we help our bodies to initiate their inherent healing processes.

We must start by paying attention to our bodies' sensations to begin awakening their senses. Usually, when asked to feel our bodies, we end up thinking about them instead of feeling them. This is because we're so used to living in our thoughts. Let's understand this better by going through a quick experience together.

First, take a moment to think about your hands. What do you see in your mind's eye? Perhaps you visualize the familiar shape of your hands that you're used to seeing. Thoughts about your hands, such as their appearance, any accessories you wear on your fingers or wrists, and any discomfort you might feel, such as arthritis, may also come to mind.

Now, close your eyes and bring your attention to your hands. Notice the sensations you feel. You might sense warmth, coldness, tingling (especially if your hands often ache), or the feeling of your hand touching another part of your body, like your knee if it's resting there. Or you might not feel anything at all, which is okay, too.

Next, clap your hands together for one minute, paying close attention to the sensations in your hands as you do so. You may notice the feeling of your palms coming together and the movement of your arms and elbows.

After you've finished clapping, gently place your hands on your knees, close your eyes, and take a moment to observe how your hands feel. You may notice a warmth spreading through them, a gentle tingling sensation, or even a subtle deepening of your breath. If you experience joint pain, you might feel some discomfort.

The first exercise involves recalling information about the body that you've stored in your mind, which essentially means delving into memories from the past. The second and third exercises focus on directly observing the sensations of your body in the present moment. It's not about thinking; it's about feeling.

In particular, the third exercise encourages you to pay attention to the sensations that arise in your body while you move. This straightforward approach is the simplest, most effective, and most direct way to awaken your body's senses. You'll find detailed guidance on how to practice this in the upcoming sections of this book.

The Meaning of Being in the Body

Let me offer you an analogy. Imagine your body as your home, and your mind as a resident of that home. However, your mind tends to wander outside rather than stay put. When something grabs its attention outside, your mind follows it, leaving the house behind for days, months, or even years.

While your mind is away, your body is left like an unattended house, neglected and gathering problems over time. Dust settles on the table, and items pile up haphazardly in the closet. It all becomes so chaotic that locating anything is a struggle. You return home to find it in disarray, and you are reluctant to deal with the mess. So, you leave the house again and go elsewhere.

When your mind is disconnected from your body for too long, negative consequences arise. Your body weakens, and your health suffers. You're putting in a lot of effort, but you still feel unsatisfied. Life loses its vitality, joy, and passion, leaving you feeling stagnant. You sense a lack of authenticity, feeling like an impostor in your own life.

To exit that state, you need to return to your home, bringing your mind back to your body. Your body and mind must be connected. Being in your body means consciously anchoring your mind within it and staying there. Your body is always in the present moment; it cannot dwell in the past or future. Conversely, your mind often wanders between past and future thoughts. Just like a balloon drifting from place to place with the wind, your mind constantly moves from one place to another, carried by the moment's stimulation.

By consciously feeling and remaining in your body, your mind stays in the present moment, where healing can happen. The past has already passed, and the future has not yet arrived; they exist only as memories and projections in your mind. The only time for change and healing is right now. By bringing your mind into your body and attuning to its sensations, you gain clarity on what's happening in your body, mind, and life.

When you engage with your body in the present moment, you process past experiences more effectively. This is because you are less likely to be overwhelmed by strong emotions and thoughts that can cloud your judgment. Viewing past experiences more objectively allows you to learn from them and grow, rather than remaining stuck in old patterns and pains. This awareness also helps you shape your future. You make decisions that align with your goals and values by staying anchored in the body and focusing on the present moment while letting go of past regrets and future anxieties. This approach can lead to a more positive and fulfilling life.

Veronica's Story

Veronica, a woman in her late thirties who attended my workshop in Colorado, struggled with severe insomnia. Her lack of proper sleep left her feeling dazed and fatigued even during waking hours. Her insomnia began about a year before she crossed paths with me. She had been diligently working on an online magazine for her company but ended up overworking, especially when she decided to create a special edition for the company's 10th anniversary. Her workload skyrocketed, leading her to work late into the night and spend over 10 hours a day in front of the computer. With irregular sleep and eating habits, she experienced rapid weight gain and a tightness in her chest. Despite these signs, she didn't worry much, believing herself to be healthy.

Then one night, she suddenly woke up feeling stiffness and tingling in the back of her neck. As she opened her eyes, her breathing became extremely fast, and she felt dizzy. Cold sweat poured down her face, and she began to feel anxious, something she had never experienced before in her life. A fear came over her as if she was about to die. Shocked, she rushed into the living room.

It was a panic attack. Following that, she began experiencing it two or three times a month. While she could easily fall asleep before, she suffered from insomnia after the panic attacks started. The shock of the initial attack made it difficult for her to return to sleep, as she dreaded the possibility of another episode.

Veronica's panic attack pattern is as follows: she continuously revisits the moment her panic attack first occurred and recalls the sense of unreality she experienced. Then, her thoughts fluctuate: "Why did I suddenly feel disoriented? Was I dreaming?" Her thoughts veer to extremes. "Do I have a fatal illness? Is the doctor deceiving me? Am I losing my mind?" As she dwells on these thoughts, she feels her heart sink, her anxiety escalating like a fountain, triggering another panic attack.

Veronica explained, "If I try to suppress these negative thoughts, thinking they're the problem and shouldn't be there, they become stronger. I just can't break free from this cycle of negative and depressing thoughts."

I encouraged Veronica to stop attempting to change her thoughts with more thoughts. Instead, I guided her to focus on feeling the physical sensations of her body by shaking and tapping it. Through this process, her thoughts naturally diminished, and her mind found rest. As she continued practicing this focus on her physical sensations, her anxiety and fear gradually decreased. After four months of training, she slept through the night and was free from panic attacks.

Returning to Your Body

Our bodies are not merely physical entities composed of skin, bones, organs, and cells; they encompass much more. They also harbor our thoughts, emotions, memories, and feelings, storing a wealth of information within them. Within this complex system lies our truth, our true nature, our authentic selves. Our bodies possess all the senses necessary to recall and experience who we really are. This is the natural intelligence and wisdom our bodies possess.

Occasionally, we catch a fleeting glimpse of the infinite nature within our bodies. In those moments, we feel open, expanded, and deeply fulfilled. However, more often than not, we find ourselves grappling with discomfort in our bodies, as well as with unsupportive thoughts and emotions. Mistakenly, we identify these experiences as our true nature. Over time, they shape our self-identity, habits, and personality, leading us to believe that this is who we are.

By awakening your senses and being present in your body, you peel away the layers of what does not truly define you, one by one. As you remain focused on your physical sensations, your awareness naturally expands, allowing you to become attuned not only to your bodily experiences but also to your emotions. Moreover, you gain insight into the patterns of your thoughts, feelings, and behaviors, fostering greater self-awareness.

Through this process, you begin to see yourself as separate from your thoughts, feelings, and actions, rather than being identified with them. You come to understand that your thoughts, feelings, and actions are not inherent to you but rather experiences you undergo. This state of awareness is known as "observer consciousness." In this state, as observers of our experiences, we acknowledge,

"My body is not me, but mine." Similarly, we can realize, "My mind is not me, but mine."

Throughout our lives, we're surrounded by countless events and experiences. No matter how well we manage ourselves and our thoughts, we can't fill our lives only with positivity and joy. Unforeseen and uncontrollable events, often accompanied by suffering, are inevitable. However, when we awaken to our body's senses and truly inhabit it, we develop a greater awareness of ourselves. This allows us to avoid identifying too closely with such experiences and our feelings of pain. It liberates us from the illusion that our pain is permanent and essential. While we acknowledge pain as part of life, we avoid becoming trapped by it.

In the previous chapter, I mentioned that even though our lives seem focused on the physical, they're also deeply spiritual. I want to emphasize that our spiritual journey is intimately connected with the physical. We can't pursue spirituality without considering our bodies and physical existence. Our bodies are where awareness, growth, and change occur. Through our bodies, we access our limitless potential, the power of the present moment, and the reality of our infinite nature. Every healing journey is about coming home to our true selves and is also about returning to our bodies.

CHAPTER 3

HARNESSING THE POWER OF ENERGY

When you focus deeply on your body and pay attention to how it feels, you'll start to experience your senses becoming sharper. This process awakens a subtle, often overlooked sense within us—the capacity to feel energy. Recognizing and engaging with this energy can enhance your healing process, taking your journey of self-discovery to a whole new level.

For thousands of years, many cultures have recognized the existence of this subtle energy. For example, it is known as *chi* or *qi* in Eastern Asian traditions and as *prana* in yoga. Native Americans have various names for the power running through all natural objects, and the ancient Greeks spoke of *pneuma*. Even in the West, before the Industrial Revolution, people referred to *elan vital*, the mysterious energy running through and maintaining all life. For those who practice meditation, yoga, tai chi, or qigong, using this energy for health and healing might already be a familiar experience. However, many people who have heard of this concept haven't experienced it directly and think of it only in abstract terms.

Concepts of energy also appear in popular culture, where it is shown in fantastical scenarios—like the mystical powers in *Doctor Strange*, the Force wielded by the Jedi in the *Star Wars* franchise, or even the energy balls seen in Pokémon cards and games. While these stories are entertaining flights of fantasy, the use of subtle energy for healing is not fictional. It is practical and grounded in centuries-old traditions.

We often use the term "energy" in various contexts in our daily lives, whether talking about the electricity powering our gadgets or describing someone's level of vitality and spirit. You might say someone is "full of energy" or complain about feeling "low energy." This everyday use of the word hints at its broader significance in Eastern philosophy, medicine, and martial arts, where energy is seen as a critical life force.

However, the energy that I refer to is more fundamental than the everyday energy associated with mood or activity levels. It's the essence of life itself, flowing through everything in the universe, including us. This energy circulates within our bodies just as blood or lymph does, keeping us alive, moving, and communicating with the world around us. While it's a physical sensation that can be felt, it goes beyond visible dimensions or forms. Energy is the bridge that connects our body and mind and links the visible and the invisible.

If this idea of energy is new to you, I encourage you to keep an open mind. Everything I've explained will make sense as you learn more and experience it for yourself.

My Experience with Energy

During a time in my life when I was deeply depressed, I found myself drawn to the practice of extreme sports. On the outside, my life seemed perfect—a beautiful house and a supporting husband, a rewarding job, and a lifestyle many would envy. But inside, I felt an overwhelming sense of emptiness and a constant worry about living up to others' expectations. I could never fully relax or feel at ease.

I found my escape in activities like mountain biking, snowboarding, and particularly through rock climbing. These sports demanded my full attention; for example, rock climbing required me to concentrate solely on my next move and my breathing, pushing aside any other worries. In these moments, I felt free and alive, unburdened by the usual mental weight. My passion for rock climbing grew so strong that I moved from Florida to Colorado to pursue it further.

I was introduced to energy practices through a friend who was not only my rock-climbing partner but also happened to become a Body & Brain Yoga instructor. One day, she expressed her anxiety about teaching her first class early in the morning, fearing no one would attend. To support her, I promised to be there.

Despite her nerves as a first-time instructor, that class was eye-opening for me. When my friend guided us on how to sense energy, I immediately connected with it, feeling intense sensations.

It reminded me of the focus and presence I felt during rock climbing, but it was also a very different experience, one that moved me deeply.

Whenever I connected with this energy, I felt an incredible sense of lightness, freedom, and expansiveness. It's difficult to articulate fully, but it felt like a part of me was finding its voice, offering me a deep sense of peace, stability, and joy that I had never known before. It was akin to being enveloped in a warm embrace or standing in a vast field that penetrated all of creation.

When I focused on my breathing, tuning into this energy, it felt as if a heavy weight was lifted off my shoulders, making my breathing effortlessly deeper. Discovering the beauty and power in the simple act of my lungs filling and quietly releasing air was a revelation. It was like my whole body was breathing, expanding and contracting without any boundaries. In that moment, I felt an overwhelming sense of vitality and gratitude for the gift of life. Later, I realized I was connecting more deeply with my body and true self through energy.

Energy and Self-Healing

As someone with a biotech background familiar with traditional scientific concepts, I initially struggled to accept the idea of energy healing. But, through my personal experiences and seeing many others find healing through energy practices, I began to understand how energy profoundly influences healing. Now it's at the heart of what I share with others.

I want to introduce you to the fundamental energy healing principles essential for the upcoming journey. Over the next 21 days, you will delve into practices grounded in these vital insights.

1. Our bodies have a built-in, perfect energy system.

2. This energy system keeps us balanced and healthy.

3. Disruptions in this energy system lead to physical, emotional, and mental issues.

4. Restoring this energy system can rebalance us and resolve these issues.

This idea of energy healing isn't new; it's deeply rooted in Eastern traditions that date back thousands of years. Across Asia, the idea of universal energy flowing through all living things, including our bodies, is widely acknowledged. This principle forms the foundation of practices such as Eastern medicine, qigong, tai chi, and martial arts. These traditions teach that our bodies contain specific energy centers and pathways facilitating energy flow. To address health problems, Eastern medicine uses acupuncture, acupressure, moxibustion, and herbal remedies to target this energy system, aiming to restore balance.

The Hindu tradition in India has also significantly contributed to the understanding of energy. According to this tradition, we have seven vital energy centers called chakras. Acting like regulating sensors for our bodies, chakras are closely connected to our physical, mental, and spiritual health. Each chakra impacts different areas of our well-being, and keeping them balanced is crucial for our overall harmony and vitality.

Unlocking our body's energy systems isn't just reserved for a select few—it's accessible to everyone. With the right knowledge and training, anyone can learn to activate, balance, and strengthen their energy. These abilities are already within us; all it takes is some learning and practice to tap into this incredible potential.

Activating Your Energy

Our bodies come equipped with a complete energy system, yet many of us are unaware of its presence. And among those who do know, a good number aren't sure how to use it effectively. Additionally, everyday factors like stress, poor lifestyle choices, and negative emotions and thoughts can disrupt our energy system.

Good health is characterized by smooth energy circulation throughout the body, maintaining balance and harmony. Many contemporary health issues are closely linked to stress and our mental state. Stress and mental disarray can throw our body's energy off balance. Mental stress impacts our physical well-being almost immediately after it begins in our minds.

Undesirable mental states such as stress, anxiety, or irritability can create negative energy states within the body, disrupting the natural flow of energy and potentially leading to various illnesses. Moreover, this build-up of negative energy in your body can further increase stress levels in your mind. It can also lead to mental health issues, such as depression or insomnia, creating a cycle of negative impact on both your mental and physical well-being.

I've witnessed numerous instances of natural healing where individuals simply open their energy pathways, allowing energy to flow through them and alleviating symptoms as if they had never existed. Most energy practices involve a mix of physical and mental exercises, all focused on bringing in fresh energy to break through stagnant blockages and bring balance and harmony back to the body. And it all begins with activating energy in your body.

Your body has energy centers, which you can think of as power plants and batteries that store your energy. Just as your laptop or phone shows a blinking light or turns red when the battery is low, signaling it's time to recharge, your body has its own way of alerting you when your energy is low or out of balance. You might feel this through physical tiredness, mental fog, emotional upset, or other unusual symptoms. These are your body's signals, telling you it's time to pay attention and recharge and rebalance your energy.

The lower and more blocked your body's energy becomes, the more health problems you tend to face. Imagine feeling tired all the time, getting stressed out easily, or feeling overwhelmed by emotions like anger or sadness that seem ready to burst out. This is a sign your body's energy is low and stuck. When you're in this state, you can't handle the changes and challenges of life well, and you may get caught in a cycle of negativity.

Yolessa Lawrinnce, an expert in energy healing and intuition based in Sedona and featured in the *Love Heals* film, shared the following insight: "Healing takes a huge amount of energy. So, one of the reasons that people often can't resolve their conflicts or heal is that they don't have enough energy emotionally, mentally, or physically." As she explained, low energy hinders proper healing.

In many people's healing journeys, I've encountered a common struggle: the feeling of being hopelessly "stuck." It's like navigating through life with chains holding you back, repeating the same motions day in and day out, yet going nowhere. This sense of being stuck—whether it's in your body, mind, emotions, or spirit—indicates that your body's energy is also stuck. This energetic blockage acts as a barrier, impeding your ability to move forward and inhibiting growth. Yet, there is a way to break free: the first step is to activate your energy.

Through practices that activate energy, you can feel the energy flowing and moving inside you. By consistently nurturing the sensation of energy and following it, you can break free from feeling stuck. This experience is very real and tangible. As the blocked energy in your body starts to flow once more, it's like being stuck in the mud and finally managing to lift your foot and step forward. You'll feel as though a heavy stone has been lifted from your chest, allowing you to breathe deeply and freely again. You will discover energy you never knew you had before—energy that's potentially limitless.

Many individuals who are dealing with chronic pain or illness feel weak, so they try to conserve energy by reducing physical activity. However, this approach only causes their energy to stagnate further. As a result, they find themselves utterly drained to the point of physical, mental, and emotional exhaustion. However, when they start learning to feel and activate their energy, they realize they aren't as powerless as they thought. In fact, they find a surprising amount of energy and strength inside themselves they never knew was there.

Anna, who previously discussed her newfound connection with her body, shares her experience with energy from the retreat:

"With my medical condition, I'm supposed to get a lot of rest; I nap for two hours daily. I don't do much because I'm advised against it, and I often don't feel well. Then we did this energy thing, and an energy shift started to happen. I could feel a massive amount of energy in my hands, and I felt powerful. When I was asked to place my hands on my heart and bring that energy in, it felt like a new depth of power came to me. There's something about this energy I don't understand. The entire week, I skipped my naps. Normally, I experience many arrhythmias daily—rhythm changes in my heart. This week, I had almost none."

Anna came to a profound awareness that energy is constantly moving throughout her body and that she has the power and personal strength to feel and use this energy as she needs. She knows that focusing on listening to what her body is telling her and using her body's natural energy brings about many different layers and types of healing.

Feeling energy brings a sense of strength, freedom, openness, connection, and growth. It reveals that your true self is boundless and unlimited. Energy helps you experience this reality, showing you what it means to feel yourself authentically, beyond just thoughts and emotions.

You can go beyond your usual self-image and connect with the limitless part of yourself. Energy acts as the bridge for this deeper connection. That's why focusing on feeling energy and cultivating this ability is crucial in your healing journey. In the practice part of this book, you'll learn how to sense this energy and use it to heal yourself.

Chad's Story

Chad had been living every day with constant pain due to fibromyalgia. Simple actions that most people take for granted, like shaking hands, caused him unbearable pain, as if a robot were crushing his hand. Even tasks like opening a bottle of water turned into major hurdles. There were nights when the pain was so bad he found himself rolling in bed, screaming and crying.

For years, Chad was on a quest to understand the relentless pain that shadowed his life. He has endured severe physical trauma—six knee surgeries, a shoulder reconstruction, and two serious back injuries. But beyond the physical issues, Chad carried deep emotional wounds from his childhood and other traumas. It was a long journey before he realized that these emotional issues were translating into physical pain in his body.

The intensity of Chad's pain reached such high levels that even his doctor was shocked. This situation led Chad, a believer in natural healing methods, to start taking medication for relief, which he had wanted to avoid. Yet, Chad was committed to finding healing through natural means, practicing qigong, meditating, and adjusting his diet.

His pursuit of healing was solitary, and he spent hours poring over hundreds of books and documentaries, all from a small town in Mexico. Two years ago, he remarkably reduced his pain and took his last pill, defying predictions that he might need medication for life. But a few months ago, his old childhood traumas resurfaced, causing his pain to flare up again, bringing anxiety and fear with it. That's why he joined the Love Heals Retreat.

Chad describes an unforgettable moment during the retreat: "We were guided through a short session of tapping and energy meditation on the first day. That was the first time I truly understood and felt what energy was. I had been practicing qigong for years, but everything clicked during that meditation. I could actually feel the energy flowing through me. It was both energizing and cleansing, removing the unnecessary from my body and replenishing what I needed. The next morning, I woke up, and the pain was just. . . gone. I still can't quite comprehend how it happened, but it was absolutely incredible."

But the most difficult struggle for Chad has always been his constant feeling of loneliness. As a kid, he had no one he could trust or open up to. His mother was overwhelmed with her own issues. She had her first baby at age 15, and by her early twenties, she was raising three kids. And both his dad and uncle molested him at a young age, leaving him with wounds that still hurt him to this day. He had many relationships, but none could alleviate his deep loneliness. He realized that this sense of isolation led to his struggles with drinking and other issues as he tried to fill the void of not having anyone to rely on.

Chad says, "My experiences with energy have helped me truly feel and understand myself, giving me a sense of wholeness. I've realized that, although I cherish the wonderful people in my life, I am ultimately the one I can truly depend on. I felt it was okay to be alone, to be just as I am. This realization led me to forgive my father. When he died, I just felt numb, my emotions completely shut down. Despite never receiving a hug, a kiss, or even a kind word from him, and only experiencing hurt that haunted me every night, I was able to forgive him while feeling energy. This one exercise was one of the most powerful steps in my healing journey. I understood that forgiveness isn't about him or what he did to me; it's about me letting go and choosing to live my life today."

He added, "I've endured deep physical and emotional pain and know many others have too. I feel a strong desire to help them. I've met people who had the best parents and were financially secure, yet they still harbored issues needing healing. I believe the energy practice I was lucky to experience can benefit everyone because it impacts every aspect of our lives—physical, emotional, mental, and spiritual."

* * *

Energy is a fundamental force that permeates our beings and profoundly impacts our health and well-being. When we learn to harness this energy, we can tap into a powerful source of healing and vitality. By connecting deeply with the energy that flows within and around us, we can open ourselves to a world of self-healing, wholeness, and a deeper understanding of our existence.

CHAPTER 4

EXPLORING ENERGY PRINCIPLES

Now, let's delve deeper into the transformative power of energy for healing. First, it's essential to understand fundamental principles about how energy operates within our bodies. I'll guide you through three fundamental concepts that can be game-changers for your healing journey. Mastering and integrating these concepts into your daily practices can restore balance and harmony to your energy system.

ENERGY PRINCIPLE 1:

Energy Follows Where the Mind Goes

This principle suggests that energy flows in the direction of your thoughts, impacting your body and surroundings. You might already know about the Law of Attraction, which follows this same idea: you end up attracting whatever you concentrate on with your mind.

Here's a quick exercise to demonstrate the power of directing energy through focused attention. Begin by taking a few deep breaths to relax. Next, open your hand with your left palm facing upward and fix your attention on the center of it. Visualize warmth radiating from your palm as you concentrate. Continue this visualization for a minute or two. You'll notice your palm gradually warming up. This occurs because focusing your mind on a particular area directs energy there, enhancing blood and energy circulation to your palm.

This concept is rooted in the understanding that everything, including the universe and our minds, is composed of energy. Consequently, shifts in our mental energy can have a tangible impact on our physical reality. By harnessing the power of focused attention, you can tap into the limitless energy of the universe and direct it toward specific parts of your body or any object. Your mind's focus isn't limited by who or what the target is, nor by distance or time. You can channel love and healing energy to someone miles away or focus energy on achieving your personal goals. The key to its power lies in your intention and how deeply you concentrate.

Think of it like using a magnifying glass to focus sunlight. If you keep moving the magnifying glass, the light scatters and loses its intensity. But if you hold the magnifying glass steady, the light concentrates and can even start a fire. Similarly, when your attention wanders, its power diminishes. However, when you focus your attention, it becomes a powerful force capable of driving significant change.

Bruce Lipton, renowned for his book *The Biology of Belief* and featured in the *Love Heals* film, highlights the critical role our minds play in shaping our health and well-being. He asserts, "The mind is creating our biology," suggesting that our genetic expression is influenced not just by our DNA but also by our beliefs and environment.

He details this process by explaining, "Whatever the picture in your mind is, it's translated into complementary chemistry. So, it's like paint by numbers. The brain sees a picture, breaks it down into chemistry that matches that image, and releases it into the blood. So, the body becomes that; we become the picture." This idea mirrors the principle that where your mind goes, energy follows and suggests that by changing our minds, we can directly influence our health and life.

By getting a grip on this principle, you unlock your brain's creative potential and gain better control over your body's energy, leading to enhanced physical, mental, and emotional health. The healing power of energy is profound, but tapping into this power starts with your mind. Essentially, the depth of your desire for healing and change, along with your dedication and focus, make all the difference. The first step toward healing and change is to acknowledge their necessity. Then, you must choose to change unequivocally and with complete sincerity. You have the power to bring about healing and change, and you don't need anyone else's approval or validation to choose what's best for you. If you truly commit to it, it will become your reality.

Water Up, Fire Down

The *Love Heals* film extensively explores the Water Up, Fire Down principle, which describes the circulation of cool water energy and warm fire energy within our bodies. When in balance, cool energy moves up to the head (water up), and warm energy flows down to the lower abdomen (fire down).

According to traditional Eastern medicine, the kidneys create water energy, and the heart makes fire energy. When our body is balanced, the fire energy from the heart descends to the lower abdomen, creating warmth in that area. This warmth activates the water energy in the kidneys, causing it to rise to the brain. In turn, the water energy in the brain pushes the fire energy in the heart back down to the lower abdomen, forming a continuous circuit.

This ideal energy circulation results in a cool head and a warm belly, which is optimal for our overall health. A cool head promotes a calm and peaceful mind, enhancing concentration, judgment, and creativity. A warm abdomen ensures that our digestive, reproductive, and endocrine functions operate normally.

When this energy flow flips the wrong way, you might feel "hot-headed" and could face headaches, insomnia, anxiety, dry eyes and mouth, and an uneven heartbeat. It can also make your neck and shoulders stiff. If warm energy doesn't get to the lower abdomen, the area's energy weakens, leading to issues with digestion, reproduction, and hormones. If this reversed flow goes on for too long, it can lead to serious health issues like high blood pressure, heart attacks, autoimmune diseases, and strokes. Bruce Lipton adds insight to this concept by noting, "When we are not in harmony with nature outside and inside, we develop disease. Basically, disharmony is disease." This perspective supports the principle that optimal health is achieved through a balanced energy flow.

The Water Up, Fire Down principle is not just seen in the human body but also in nature. The sun's heat warms the earth and oceans (fire down), causing water to evaporate and rise into the sky (water up). Trees, too, thrive on this cycle, drawing water up through their roots from the ground while their leaves absorb the energy sent down from the sun.

The energy cycle of water and fire is an essential principle of life in nature. All living things thrive when water and fire energies are balanced within them. If this balance is disrupted, vitality diminishes. A natural, unblocked flow of energy in the Water Up, Fire Down state creates the optimal condition for our bodies and minds. In this state, you can perform at your best—physically, mentally, and spiritually. On days when you feel great, with a clear head, a calm mind, and an energetic body, your body's energy is in harmony, embodying the Water Up, Fire Down balance.

Water Up, Fire Down is a crucial principle in healing because many of the physical, mental, and emotional issues we face stem from disruptions in our body's energy flow. This disruption can leave us with a hot head, a tight chest, and a cold lower abdomen. These uncomfortable symptoms are our body's way of signaling a need to restore its energy balance. By recognizing these signals early and adjusting our energy flow, we can prevent these imbalances from developing into more severe health problems.

In today's world, marked by high levels of stress, maintaining the Water Up, Fire Down balance is particularly challenging. To promote healing in both our bodies and minds, it's essential that we actively work toward achieving and sustaining this optimal energy state.

Dr. Ericka Crawford, who appeared in the *Love Heals* film and was part of its production team, interviewed many individuals practicing Brain Education and its energy principles. She observes, "Over and over again, I see that being able to feel your own energetic state and having the tools to change it is the key. It gives you the power to manage your own well-being."

In the practice section, you'll engage in exercises and meditations that help you feel what Water Up, Fire Down entails firsthand. These practical tools will allow you to recognize when your body's energy balance shifts away from this ideal state. With this awareness, you'll be able to bring your energy back into balance quickly.

Energy Evolves from Physical to Emotional to Spiritual

This principle outlines the progression of energy within us, beginning at the lower energy center in our lower abdomen, advancing to the middle center in our chest, and reaching the upper center in our brain. Through this upward journey, our energy evolution guides us through the process of developing physical vitality, then emotional maturity, and finally, spiritual awakening.

The beginning of energy development is about strengthening physical power, starting with the energy center in our lower abdomen. Much like laying a solid foundation is crucial for constructing a building, activating this energy center is an essential step in energy development that shouldn't be overlooked. When this center is activated, you'll notice an increase in physical energy and a stronger resistance to illness. You'll experience a sense of being grounded, alongside enhanced vitality and stamina.

As you build physical strength, the energy in your heart's center begins to open and mature, deepening your connection with yourself, others, and the world around you. This development opens your heart to love and peace from within, enhancing your ability to navigate your emotions. In this phase, you gain a clearer understanding that, while your thoughts and emotions may bring challenges to your life, you have the power to transform them into meaningful experiences.

The final stage involves awakening the upper energy center in the head, focusing on the brain, and enhancing your spiritual growth. This is when your body, mind, and soul become integrated, allowing you to function according to your highest potential. Here, your intuition and creativity flourish, and you open your eyes to the endless potential and interconnectedness of the world. Previously, you may have felt pulled in many directions by life, but now you have a sense of direction and vision for your life.

To reach this final stage, you will learn to unify your physical, emotional, and spiritual powers energetically by aligning your thoughts, emotions, and actions. When these are not aligned, it is like three horses pulling a chariot in different directions. Despite exerting all your energy, you end up more stressed, and your efforts seem fruitless. This misalignment often leaves us feeling stuck in life.

Alan, who I encountered in Hawaii, knew he had to stop the excessive drinking that was damaging his health and relationships. Yet, emotionally, he leaned on alcohol to cope with stress and anxiety, fearing life would be unbearable without it. As a result, despite his better judgment, he fell back into his nightly drinking routine. This tug-of-war between what he knew, what he felt, and what he did trapped him in a cycle he struggled to escape.

During a period of self-reflection, Alan discovered that despite appearing kind to others, he was internally closed off. This stemmed from a deep-seated sense of betrayal after his mother abandoned him at seven years old. This betrayal led him to trust no one, always being on guard, and quick to react defensively. Alan identified this constant state of alertness as the root of his ever-present anxiety and worry. He recognized that drinking was his sole means of unwinding after stressful days. However, he also understood that this habit was isolating him, not just from others, but also from himself.

As Alan's anxiety began to lessen through energy practice, he fully committed to stop drinking excessively. This commitment was more than just a thought; it was a decision he felt with his entire being, enabling him to turn it into action. Six months into sobriety, Alan had an unexpected experience. Yielding to a friend's suggestion, he tried a sip of alcohol only to find it unbearably bitter and nauseating. It was as if his body was rejecting it. Since that moment, Alan has maintained his sobriety for four years.

When our body, mind, and soul are awakened and in sync, and our thoughts, feelings, and actions are in harmony, we reach our highest level of focus and energy use. The most effective way to align them is to base your thoughts and actions on what your true self desires. Connecting deeply with your true self helps you understand who you are and what you want deep down. This connection simultaneously activates your physical, emotional, and spiritual powers.

Bring Energy Principles to Healing

Applying these powerful energy principles to healing is simpler than it may seem. It starts with recognizing that everything, including our bodies and minds, is made of energy. When we encounter physical or mental health challenges that seem resistant to change, the solution lies in activating and shifting our energy.

The first essential step is to choose healing consciously. It's about fully committing to the desire for healing and taking tangible actions toward it. Throughout your healing journey, it's crucial to stay closely connected to your body. Remember, wherever your mind goes, energy follows. So, consistently focusing on healing and keeping your mind firmly grounded within your body directs energy where it's needed most.

Next, to restore your body to its ideal Water Up, Fire Down energy balance, you'll engage in simple methods to activate the energy throughout your entire body, focusing primarily on the energy center in the lower abdomen. This area serves as an engine and power-house for the desired energy flow within the body. By awakening your body's energy this way, you'll gain the strength to overcome any stagnant states.

Thirdly, as the energy center in your lower abdomen awakens, you also open the energy center in your chest, releasing stagnant emotion held within your body. With your heart opening, you feel the infinite love within you enveloping your entire being, expanding and deepening. This awakens the energy center in your brain, connecting you to divine energy within and around you. In this state, you are in pure love, realizing you are made of and sustained by that love. This infinite love serves as the greatest healing power you can experience.

Jin's Story

For five years, Jin struggled to conceive without success, despite trying in vitro fertilization multiple times. To make matters more challenging, she was already juggling many autoimmune disorders like chronic fatigue syndrome and Hashimoto's, falling deeper into depression with the cumulative emotional toll of failed attempts at pregnancies.

Upon her acupuncturist's suggestion, she turned to tai chi and qigong at the Body & Brain center near her. Just three months into her training, Jin discovered she had conceived naturally. Reflecting on this, she said, "I didn't start training to get pregnant. I tried everything for five years, but nothing worked, and the doctors said it was impossible, so I gave up. I just started the practice because I needed exercise that would help my health."

Jin thinks that tapping her lower abdomen with her fists supported her fertility. This exercise, a key component of the Water Up, Fire Down practice, both calmed her over-heated and stressed mind and strengthened her depleted lower energy center. Although initially skeptical, she soon noticed significant improvements in her long-standing digestive issues, as well. Motivated by these positive changes, Jin diligently increased her tapping repetitions, eventually managing 500 to 1,000 per day, a substantial leap from her initial struggle with just 100.

She shares, "In my journey to heal from health challenges and conceive, I explored various healing approaches. This included modern medical treatments like new drugs, procedures, and psychotherapy. I also tried energy healing, and many energy healers advised me to open my second chakra, but I didn't know how. I think that tapping my lower abdomen helped open this energy center, associated with my reproductive organs, aiding my fertility."

Jin learned to reconnect her mind with her body by simply tapping her lower abdomen. This brought a warm sensation to her abdomen that spread energy throughout her lower back and pelvic floor, bringing stability to her mind and helping her focus on her body. Through this process, the principle of "energy follows where the mind goes" became clear to her.

As she strengthened the energy in her lower abdomen and restored the Water Up, Fire Down energy balance through tapping and other exercises, her body became ready for pregnancy. Reflecting on her journey, she said, "I knew and believed that the body can do miraculous things, but I just didn't know how to tap into it. I finally got the hang of it, and once I learned to accept and love my body, the challenges started to melt away one by one."

Although she is still working toward full recovery, particularly with lingering hormonal issues after an exhaustive labor later in life, she feels deeply grateful for the profound transformation she has experienced. This shift not only allowed her to conceive and give birth to her daughter but to her renewed self as well.

Jin began her energy practice to exercise her tired body and mind. However, as she continued training, she gained a greater understanding of the interconnectedness of body, mind, and soul. Through her journey, she directly experienced how energy progresses from the physical realm to the emotional and eventually to the spiritual level.

Even though her husband was always supportive, and no one blamed her, Jin couldn't shake the feeling of failure for being unable to conceive. "What's wrong with me?" This thought pervasively crept into her waking thoughts.

One of Jin's breakthrough moments came when she discovered an exercise where she could completely immerse herself and move her body freely to music. This spontaneous, unrestricted movement starkly contrasted with the highly analytical, perfectionistic mindset she usually kept as an architect. "There was no need for my logical brain to tell me how to move or how stupid I may look. It was a dance for my soul and truly healing," she shares. Through this experience, she felt a profound sense of release from the tension plaguing her life.

As she delved deeper into her energy practice, she also better understood how to let go. "I've learned to let things be, not to chase after them. Once I let myself be open and stop chasing, all the things meant for me came. As an adoptee, I had lived in multiple homes, and I always tried to be perfect to earn love and acceptance. I've always lived driven by sheer willpower, embodying traits like being highly critical, exhaustively thorough, and ambitious. While these qualities helped me navigate life's challenges, they wrecked my nervous system. I now understand that being an open vessel and being vulnerable does attest to how strong you are. I'm learning to let go of my shoulders when I'm doing simple things like washing dishes." Jin adds, "Before the practice, I was living a life of searching, just constant searching. Now, I'm done with searching. I am now into not just doing part of life, but being. And it's such a relief."

* * *

The ability to change our lives, heal our bodies, and elevate our spiritual awareness is within each of us. By learning and applying universal energy principles in our daily lives, we can unlock this potential. It all starts with harnessing this energy purposefully, aiming to use it for our well-being and the highest good.

CHAPTER 5

TRANSFORMING PAIN INTO HEALING

If you're seeking healing, you are likely experiencing some form of pain. It's natural to view pain as unfavorable because it brings discomfort. This discomfort often leads us to believe that feeling pain must be fundamentally wrong.

But pain isn't inherently bad or something to fear or reject. It's our body and mind's way of telling us that something isn't right and needs our attention. It helps us understand what's going on inside us. Pain is a normal part of life, whether it's physical, emotional, or mental. It's not something we can just fix quickly and forget. Instead, it shows up in different forms when we least expect it, teaching us important lessons about ourselves. Instead of avoiding pain, we should embrace it, fully experiencing it and allowing it to guide us.

I've met many people dealing with chronic pain. Some have been battling it for years, while others face such intense daily pain that it's hard for anyone else to imagine. Take Sarah, for example. She lives with rheumatoid arthritis, and her condition makes even the most basic tasks a struggle. Her joints are so swollen and painful that even turning a doorknob or chopping vegetables can be excruciating. A casual touch from a friend can send a jolt of pain through her body. Nights are often sleepless as she tries to find a comfortable position that will ease her discomfort.

For those who endure constant pain and seek relief, I suggest rethinking their perception of pain. "Don't run away from it; learn to accept and truly feel it," I advise. Pain points out where things aren't right, so we should let it guide us to find a way to heal.

Avoiding pain won't help us overcome it. Instead, embracing and fully experiencing our pain is essential to move through it. View pain as an invaluable companion on your path to healing. Rather than pushing it away or resenting it, lean in and explore it. Accepting your pain is not resigning yourself to it; it doesn't mean it will last forever or that you can't move past it. It means acknowledging your current state of pain without fleeing from it. This acceptance is crucial to finding relief and moving beyond your pain.

This holds true not just for physical pain, but also for mental and emotional distress. Life brings many challenges and changes we can't control, often leading to deep pain. The anguish from the issues in our relationships can be as overwhelming as physical pain, driving us to our limits. It's crucial not to ignore or suppress this pain out of fear. The key is to confront your pain honestly and openly. Even though it might hurt, facing your pain without fear is the only way to start healing.

Healing is impossible without self-honesty; true healing cannot occur without it. This is the truth. When you are honest with yourself, healing follows. Therefore, instead of avoiding your pain, face it head-on. This requires bravery. Approach your pain confidently, knowing you have the courage and strength to do so. Then, see what lies within.

Body Tapping and Its Healing Process

To confront our pain head-on, we must be fully present in this very moment. This involves uniting the mind and body into one focused entity, a concept I referred to as "being in your body" in Chapter 2. One practical method to achieve this presence is Body Tapping, which helps center your attention on the now.

If you've ever found yourself tapping your shoulders or shaking your wrists after long hours at the computer, you've instinctively engaged in your body's natural way to ease pain or discomfort. These spontaneous actions reflect the body's innate ability to release tension and restore energy flow by unblocking energy pathways and activating energy points.

When you gently tap different body parts with your fist or palm, you'll notice that the spots where energy circulates freely feel good, while the spots with blocked or stagnant energy might be sore. This pain is essentially your body's way of pointing out, "There's a blockage here; it needs your attention."

At first glance, tapping might seem too simple to have much effect. Yet, it's a remarkably powerful technique. The act of tapping your body does more than just address blockages; it also triggers a range of sensations and emotional reactions, making it a multifaceted tool for self-awareness and healing.

You might start by lightly tapping across your body, perhaps somewhat skeptically, as you struggle to keep your wandering thoughts from taking over. This initial phase can feel mechanical, just touching the surface of your skin without much expectation.

If you keep up with the tapping, you'll start to notice changes. As you get into a rhythm, you might tap a bit harder without even thinking about it. This rhythmic tapping produces a steady vibration, pulling your focus further inward. The sensation goes beyond just surface contact; it penetrates deeper. Each tap resonates more strongly, moving beyond the skin to penetrate your body at the muscular and cellular levels.

As you continue this practice, you'll likely experience many physical sensations. You might feel heavy or light or notice your muscles tightening and then relaxing. Some parts of your body might feel warm, others cool, and you might feel tingly or itchy. Pain might also arise in various parts of your body, whether it's a familiar ache, a long-forgotten pain resurfacing, or discomfort in entirely new areas. This is a sign of your body's previously inactive senses coming to life.

And then, there's an emotional awakening. As you persist with tapping, emotions buried deep within start to surface. These aren't just fleeting feelings; they are raw, often intense emotions tied to memories you may have long forgotten or consciously set aside. It's like each tap unlocks a door to a room inside you that's been sealed off. Feelings of resentment, fear, sadness, and more start to surface. Encountering these emotions can be surprising, sometimes overwhelming, but they are incredibly revealing. During this phase of emotional cleansing, it's not uncommon for people to cry openly, laugh, or even scream as they release these pent-up emotions.

From this moment, tapping transforms into an exploration of your emotional and spiritual depths. With every tap, you activate the energy within, sending vibrations that ripple across your entire being. It's as if you're unlocking and releasing layers of emotional residue that have accumulated over time, clearing the way for profound inner change.

As you keep tapping, you'll move past the immediate sense of pain and the rush of thoughts and emotions. You'll reach a deeper, peaceful place inside you, full of calm, clarity, and a sense of self-love. Here, you start to see the real you, hidden away under all the noise of daily life. You'll uncover where your limiting beliefs and patterns come from—identifying specific people, places, or experiences that have shaped you. You'll also notice how these things connect to certain feelings in your body and see how they influence your everyday thoughts, emotions, and actions.

This process of tapping isn't just therapeutic; it's transformative. It brings you face-to-face with your innermost self—the pains you've avoided, the emotions you've suppressed, and the parts of yourself you've been unwilling to accept. True healing begins to blossom in the soil of self-honesty. It begins when you stop running from your pain. Transformation starts when you stop putting on a brave face or pretending that everything is fine when it isn't.

This process can be incredibly challenging. It might feel like reopening old wounds or admitting to weaknesses you've long denied. But in this confrontation lies freedom. As you acknowledge and accept these hidden aspects of yourself, you start to break free from the chains of your past. You're finally unstuck.

As you embark on your healing journey, you'll find that not only do you begin to heal, but you also discover a strength and resilience within you that perhaps you didn't know existed. This is the beauty of the healing process—it doesn't just repair the old; it transforms you into something stronger, more authentic, and more aligned with your true self.

This ties back to the energy development stages discussed in the previous chapter. Your healing journey starts physically, moves through the emotional as you delve into your feelings, and ultimately reaches the spiritual, where you discover your true essence. This entire transformation can begin with the simple act of Body Tapping. This method highlights the interconnectedness of body, mind, and soul. The energy and vibrations generated by Body Tapping stimulate all aspects of your being, fostering holistic healing. While I will introduce various healing techniques in the practice section, Body Tapping is the foundational technique I encourage you to adopt.

When engaging in the healing process with Body Tapping, view pain as a guide rather than an enemy. This mindset opens the door for profound healing. Bearing this in mind, we explore insights from Les Aria, PhD, a pain psychologist at Kaiser Permanente Medical Group, who offers a valuable perspective on managing pain.

He explains that modern science now believes the brain has a big influence on whether pain will continue or not. We often think that pain comes from a specific body part that is affected, but it actually originates in the brain, which sends out pain signals.

Dr. Aria points out how important it is to feel safe to start healing from chronic pain. He explains that healing cannot happen if the brain feels unsafe. This means your nervous system needs to feel calm and not in a state of anxiety.

He continues, "Even though I'm a pain psychologist, it sounds ridiculous, but I don't focus on changing your thinking. Unlike many of my colleagues who try to change people's thinking, what I do is calm the body first. This activates the vagus nerve, sending a message back to the brain: I am safe. Following this, the brain starts to rewire itself."

He emphasizes that the typical approach to pain needs to shift. When you're dealing with chronic medical conditions, especially chronic pain, understand that your nervous system is trying to protect you. Our nervous system uses pain as a protective signal. So, it's crucial to be kind, non-judgmental, curious, and accepting of what your pain is communicating without resistance.

He suggests addressing your pain, saying, "Come if you will, stay if you will, leave if you will. I'm not going to fight you. You're here to protect me, and I'm fully present. Whether you work with me or not, I will be here with you." This mindset fosters a sense of safety within the nervous system.

He also notes that approaching pain in this manner can transform lives. But he adds, "This is not for everyone; this is for the courageous. For healing to start, it requires you to stop fighting. It requires you to show up, and if you're not willing to show up, your pain is not willing to back off."

Dr. Aria shares powerful insights on healing. Contrary to the common belief that healing means curing or no longer experiencing discomfort, healing is, in essence, about cultivating the ability to welcome everything within us. Healing is not about eliminating something; it's about learning to relate differently to everything that appears in our lives.

Dana's Story

Dana, the protagonist of the film *Love Heals*, experienced profound healing by encountering her pain head-on. Before the retreat, Dana struggled with severe discomfort in her lower back and legs and doubted her ability to engage in the retreat's physical activities.

Surprisingly, despite ongoing discomfort, she could fully participate in all sessions, sustaining her stamina. "It was a huge awakening for me to understand that when you deeply connect with your body, it can make a real difference. It's as if the volume of the pain was turned down. It no longer had sharp edges; instead of being the loudest thing I could focus on, it ended up being in the background," she shares.

At one point, Dana suddenly experienced a wave of unexpected anger while tapping on her chest and solar plexus. This caught her off guard because she had never considered herself an angry person or someone who harbored unexpressed anger.

"I've gone through a lot of pain, including almost every form of abuse and trauma imaginable," she says. The energy activation through tapping allowed her to finally feel the anger from the numerous abuses and traumas she endured throughout her life. She realized she had to acknowledge this anger before she could let it go completely.

While she thought she had already forgiven those who harmed her physically, emotionally, and even sexually through her previous work, her body told a different story. "I don't think I could have let go of the anger, feelings of self-betrayal from not speaking my truth or not standing up for myself, and all that suppression in any other way than by deeply connecting with my body," she recalls.

As this unfolded, Dana was overwhelmed by an incredible surge of energy coursing through her body. "It was so open and light. Instead of mentally processing the things that I've gone through in my life, there was just pure release, accompanied by tears," she describes. It was both beautiful and painful but utterly worthwhile.

Her journey through deep pain and darkness awakened something vital within her. Despite the challenges, it led her to a place of authenticity and a deep level of self-compassion, acceptance, and love. She stated she wouldn't change her past or the path she took because it shaped her into who she is now.

Dana has come to understand that healing is not a destination where everything suddenly becomes perfect. Instead, the journey of healing is where the real answers lie. It's about staying on that path, not giving up, accepting the parts of ourselves that seem so broken, and understanding that being imperfect is part of the human experience.

Dana reflects, "During the retreat, the consistent message I received was not about if I'll heal or when I'll move past this part of my life, but rather about recognizing that I am already in the process of healing and helping others do the same. I thought my life would begin when the pain ended. In reality, my life began when the pain started."

It Gets Worse Before It Gets Better

I need to offer a word of caution at this stage. The path toward healing—confronting your pain instead of avoiding it, and fully experiencing it, both physically and emotionally—might not always be pleasant or smooth. There will be moments when it becomes tough and deeply unsettling. In such times, it's common to feel worried and want to shut the door you've courageously opened. Yet, it's precisely during these challenging periods that we must summon our deepest reserves of self-compassion and maintain unwavering hope for healing. These difficult feelings are not signs of failure but rather indicators that healing is actively taking place within your body and mind.

In the healing process, it's normal for things to feel worse before they get better. This happens as we shift from ignoring or numbing our pain to fully acknowledging it. Our senses become sharper, bringing to light the full extent of our discomfort. Experts in the field often refer to this phase as a "healing crisis."

When you start on the path to healing, hoping for quick relief is natural. However, you might initially feel even worse. As your awareness sharpens, you become acutely aware of the underlying issues you've overlooked in your body and mind. Physically, this means your body is starting to get rid of built-up fatigue or toxins, leading to symptoms like headaches, joint pain, and tiredness. Emotionally, you might begin to recall old wounds or traumatic experiences you thought you'd moved past, and you might reexperience them in the form of depression, anxiety, worry, or anger.

During healing, we must let go of the burdens we've been holding on to. Sometimes these things are buried deep in our subconscious, and we are unaware we are still holding on to them until they resurface. Think about how you feel the day after you've had too much to drink: it's awful. Your body tries to get rid of the alcohol, leading to bad headaches and feeling sick. Sometimes, you might even throw up. But after all that, you feel lighter and more at ease. In the same way, during healing, you'll start to notice all the unhealthy things coming out of your system. This is all part of the healing process.

As we awaken our senses and activate our energy, we become sensitive to the underlying physical tensions, emotional scars, and negative patterns we've been ignoring. It might feel heavy before it feels light. You'll have to face some darkness before you find the light inside you. However, this phase of heaviness and darkness is a pathway to freedom, openness, love, and healing. Don't retreat from these experiences. They aren't your defining traits, nor are they permanent. Embrace this period as an opportunity for growth. Instead of pulling away, lean into yourself, embracing your journey toward healing and self-discovery.

When your beloved child cries over a wound, you wouldn't silence them or leave them to cope alone. Instead, you'd draw closer, examine the injury, offer comfort, and seek ways to heal it. Apply this same kindness and proactive approach to your own pain.

Detachment and Disconnection

Our minds are adept at avoiding pain, constantly seeking ways to escape discomfort. This tendency often results in a disconnect between the mind and body. Therefore, it's essential to keep your mind engaged with your body intentionally. If your mind wanders during practices like tapping, your body may go through the motions without experiencing genuine healing.

Disconnection happens when your body and mind are out of sync. Your body is physically present, but your mind is wandering elsewhere. While your body engages in an activity like tapping, your mind remains disengaged, merely going through the motions without truly connecting to the sensations that give the practice depth and significance. In this state, you're prone to attachment and resistance, becoming entangled in your thoughts and emotions as if they define your entire being. These factors can hold you back, making it challenging to release and move forward. The solution is to actively move your body while also paying close attention to the sensations you're feeling.

Inside all of us, there's an innate wisdom, a sense of who we really are. This deep insight is always there within our reach. Through the healing process, you begin to connect with this inner truth. You discover that you are part of a continuous flow of energy, a part of something much larger than your everyday self.

This truth is always within us, even when we're not fully aware of it. Our everyday selves might not always pay attention to it, but the deeper, spiritual part of us always knows it's there. So, even if sometimes your body and mind feel disconnected, keep practicing and paying attention to your body. Keeping up with this practice will support your healing by promoting a balanced energy flow, helping your mind better manage pain.

In this process, it's vital to maintain your awareness and connect with the healer within. Healing begins by recognizing the areas that need healing. Change starts to happen when you notice discomfort in your body or patterns in your thoughts, emotions, and behaviors that you haven't noticed before.

Focusing on the discomfort and pain in both your body and mind directs energy to those areas. And where energy flows, change follows. Remember the principle from the previous chapter: "Energy follows where the mind goes." Your awareness acts like a magnet, drawing the necessary healing energy to the areas of your body and mind that need it the most.

True healing begins when you're genuinely connected with your experiences, not just going through the motions. It happens when your body and mind harmonize, and you're fully immersed in the present moment. In this state, you're surrounded by energy and vibrations that foster a profound connection with your innermost self, revealing your deepest truths.

Katriana's Story

Katriana had been relying on medication to manage her anxiety, panic attacks, and depression for two years. She didn't want to depend on medication and was seeking a way out of her anxious mind when she came to the retreat featured in the film.

Reflecting on her experience, Katriana shared, "I didn't realize how desensitized I was; there was so much pain in my body, and that was just mind-blowing to me. It was really powerful to bring the pain up and be with it instead of running away. When I did that, my whole body just started tingling and experienced an enormous amount of release. When I went into the tapping exercises and all of that, I just felt so grounded in my body, and my heart has opened immensely." She continued, "There had been this nervous energy in my chest all the time before I came. Now it's gone. I'm just so grateful because it feels so good. It feels like I've come home to myself, and I am not going to leave myself again."

Following the retreat, Katriana was able to cut her antidepressant medication in half. "There have been times where I've dipped a little bit. Then I realized, oh, I haven't been getting into my body today," she remarked.

Pain Is Not Me

I want to emphasize this one more time: when you begin your healing journey, expect to face moments of heaviness, darkness, and pain. It's important to understand, though, that these feelings are not you. Rather than identifying with them, detach and observe them from a distance. Remember, you are not the pain itself; you are the one experiencing it and observing it.

The challenges and suffering we encounter in life provide us with opportunities for deep reflection and growth, leading to true healing and self-discovery. While the frustration and pain of being stuck can feel overwhelming, they can also catalyze change. When we are confronted with doubts about the direction of our lives or the authenticity of our existence, we may experience deep emptiness and fear. However, this moment of uncertainty can propel us to embark on a journey of self-discovery, to uncover our true selves, and to clarify our genuine desires in life.

Therefore, when suffering, pain, and questions arise, it's crucial not to ignore or push them away out of fear of disrupting your life. The key is to bravely face the pain, acknowledge it, and fully engage with it without becoming the pain itself. By distinguishing yourself from the pain, you gain control over your healing process.

Taleaha's Story

Taleaha's healing journey, highlighted in the film *Love Heals*, shows us how powerful it can be to accept and face our deepest pains.

Since adolescence, she has always experienced joint pain, constantly feeling achy bones and waking up feeling older than she should. Whenever she engaged in any sort of strenuous work, it put her body in pain. Medical doctors told her there wasn't a cure for what she was dealing with and to just get used to it.

As a participant in the Love Heals Retreat, Taleaha started to realize the root of her problem: her unstable childhood. When she was 12, her mother became seriously ill and was struggling with alcoholism until she passed away at the age of 59. She describes her realization, "I didn't have a good relationship with my mom. It was really shaky, lacking the stability I craved. This idea of having so much joint pain struck me. If you think about your joints, they're kind of your stability and your foundation. Maybe that's why I started feeling all this joint pain."

During the meditation, she saw herself as a child, experiencing all these traumas without any way to process them. She could see herself packing them away in her body for the sake of her own survival. Throughout her life, she'd been looking everywhere to feel secure, but it always seemed just out of reach. She realized that only one person in the world could provide the stability she was craving, and it was herself.

She now reflects, "I realized I've been running away from my pain because I didn't want to be like my mom. My mom was in constant pain and always complained about it. But it dawned on me that I've literally been running right into what I feared this whole time. I was becoming my pain. I've been walking around really numb, trying to cut the pain off from my life."

The idea that "my pain is not me but mine" completely transformed her view of her pain. She states, "Now I feel like I can do something about it. It's not that I don't have the pain anymore or I'm not feeling the pain, but now I have something to do to support it. With this realization, I felt so strong. I don't know if I've ever felt this powerful, strong. And it's not just physical strength."

So often, intergenerational trauma is passed down the line of descendants with nothing to stop it, and it festers and grows with each passing generation. Through her energy work, Taleaha was able to take full ownership of the pain she was storing within her body, ultimately transcending it. She now tells herself, "Now, I'm talking to my pain, I feel you, but I'm not owned by you. How can I take care of you?"

CHAPTER 6

RELEASING TRAPPED EMOTIONS

As we bring our attention to our bodies and tune into their sensations, we uncover the pain and discomfort stored within us. Addressing these feelings directly, rather than avoiding them, starts a profound purification process in which we face our emotions head-on.

We often view emotions as intangible phenomena that happen solely in our minds. Yet, emotions are intensely physical. Our emotions manifest through our bodies. How do you know you're angry? Perhaps you've felt an intense, fiery energy bubbling up in your chest as your muscles clench, your face tightens, and your breath shortens. In the heat of anger, your whole body might even tremble. Now, recall a moment of joy. You likely felt a warmth spreading through your chest, your step becoming lighter, and a spontaneous smile brightening your face. Emotions are not just mental states; they are full-bodied experiences.

Whenever you feel an emotion, it sparks communication between your brain and body. Whether you're happy, sad, or angry, this interaction can alter your heartbeat and breathing patterns and cause shifts in your posture, facial expressions, and muscle tension. Every emotion has a physical side to it.

Our bodies and minds are closely connected, always talking to each other. Eastern medicine believes this connection is vital to our health and provides a unique viewpoint on our physical health and emotional well-being. Western medicine usually sees problems like depression and anxiety as problems of brain functionality and thus prescribes medication to adjust brain chemistry.

But Eastern medicine sees it differently, viewing emotions as more than just the product of the brain. Feelings are connected to the rest of our body and related to specific organs. In this approach, treatments for mental health focus on fixing energy imbalances in the body. Take my friend Daniel, an Asian medicine practitioner, as an example. When he helps someone with depression, he targets energy points connected to the lungs and liver using acupuncture and qigong movements.

The energy practices you'll encounter align closely with Eastern medicine's holistic views of emotions. It's crucial to involve your body actively to release and manage your emotions. It's not enough to attempt to shift our mindset; you must also work directly with the physical sensations and energies associated with your emotions.

The Importance of Emotions

In many parts of our society, expressing emotions is not widely encouraged, and the value of emotions is often overlooked. Common sayings like, "Boys don't cry," or, "That person is too emotional," mirror this sentiment. This mindset isn't just present in public spaces; it's common within families, too. When someone tries to share deep feelings, they might be met with a dismissive response like, "Save it for your therapy session." This kind of response typically arises from discomfort and fear when confronting difficult emotional distress.

Emotions aren't just drama-makers in our lives. In making decisions, we often assume we're guided by logic and reason. Yet, our emotions and feelings significantly influence our choices. It's easier to choose something when it feels right in our hearts, not just because it makes sense in our heads. Experts believe our emotional responses are not random but have evolved as a survival tool. In essence, emotions are fundamental to our well-being.

Emotions are as vital to our existence as our lungs breathing and heart beating. They are a fundamental, universal part of being human. Just as life cannot continue without breath or a heartbeat, it cannot flourish without the full spectrum of emotions. Joy, happiness, and love, often seen as positive, along with anger, sadness, and fear, typically viewed as unfavorable, are all essential for our survival. The absence of fear would have left our ancestors vulnerable to predators, while a lack of sadness would impair our ability to connect with and understand others. Emotions, like breaths or heartbeats, are not inherently positive or negative; they are simply a part of us. Ignoring or suppressing emotions can lead to severe physical and mental health challenges.

When we hold back our feelings, they don't just disappear; they can linger in our bodies, leading to chronic stress, tension, and even physical pain. This unresolved emotional turmoil expresses itself within our body, activating the stress response intended for short-term threats. When the stress response is kept active, as though we're in constant danger, serious health issues like high blood pressure, heart problems, and mental health struggles such as anxiety and depression may arise.

In the film *Love Heals*, Dr. David Hanscom, a spine surgery specialist, explains that this type of chronic, low-level stress is a primary contributor to chronic pain and disease. The ongoing, simmering stress gradually undermines our health. Dr. Hanscom also points out a connection between chronic pain and emotions, noting, "Research uncovered that 90 percent of people with chronic pain still harbor anger toward either the person or the situation that initially caused their pain. More revealing, however, is the fact that the person they are most angry with is themselves. Whatever you decide to hold on to in the past keeps your nervous system fired up."

Ericka's Story

The narrative of Ericka clearly shows how emotions can affect physical health, especially pain.

She was close to qualifying for the Olympic trials in discus throwing right before her senior year of college. Unfortunately, she injured her knee badly during a routine ten-mile run, requiring surgery and halting her pursuit of Olympic dreams. Having already undergone two knee surgeries for previous injuries, the doctor suggested she stop throwing the discus and never run again if she wants to preserve her knee enough to walk by the time she reaches fifty. Unable to run, Ericka turned to swimming and biking to stay active.

Twelve years later, while getting ready for a big hundred-mile bike ride, Ericka's old knee pain came back. She went through two more knee surgeries and was constantly in pain, taking pain relievers to try to manage it. She remembers feeling really low, especially when she had to use the elevator instead of the stairs to get to her second-floor office.

Her massage therapist, whom she had been seeing weekly for five years just to be able to walk, suggested she try a mind-body practice. Ericka discovered a Body & Brain center nearby and began to feel better after a few classes.

Her breakthrough came at a retreat in Sedona, where she tried Brain Wave Vibration, a technique that opens up the body's energy channels. She connected deeply with the movement and felt the energy flowing through her body. "As I focused on relieving the pain in my left knee, a sudden rush of sadness and guilt hit me in the pit of my stomach. And then, all of a sudden, this huge amount of anger rose from my knee up through my leg, up through my spine, and out the top of my head, and I screamed as this happened," she recalls.

As if a cloud had been lifted, she saw the source of her knee pain with startling clarity. Childhood memories flooded back, each echoing the words of religious leaders who had made her feel unworthy.

Calmness washed over her, and clarity emerged. She had relentlessly pushed herself to be the best at everything she did to feel "worthy enough." "How could I feel that way?" she marveled. "I have a loving partner, a successful career, friends and family who love me, and material abundance. How could I still feel not good enough?"

Another realization struck like lightning. She had inflicted her own pain and stress by perpetually seeking to be "good enough." She saw with sharp clarity how this one belief, buried deep within her subconscious, had shaped her entire life.

Tears streamed down her face once she made this connection, an extraordinary sense of peace filled her body, and amazingly, the pain in her knee was released! She could walk without pain for the first time in years and stopped taking medication altogether.

Unlocking Emotional Release

Over and over, my experiences have underscored the critical importance of processing emotions for healing. That's why I prioritize time for participants to express and release their feelings at the Love Heals Retreat or any other workshop I lead. Seeing the profound impact on mental and physical health has convinced me of this practice's essential role in healing.

Since our society often discourages expressing emotions, many naturally withdraw from difficult feelings. However, genuine healing demands that we do the opposite: rather than fleeing from our emotions, we must face them directly, step into them, and see what lies beneath them.

Exploring emotions is hard work; it takes a lot of energy, courage, and patience. Like pain, emotions are our body's way of sending important messages. However, too often, we overlook these signals, dismissing them as we might with a swift dose of painkillers for physical pain.

This approach to releasing emotions is similar to how we dealt with pain before, accepting rather than denying or resenting them. When a strong emotion comes up, it's common to try pushing it away immediately instead of facing it. Your mind might look for external distractions to avoid confronting these intense feelings inside you.

So, when your mind starts looking for distractions, you need a reliable anchor to keep it grounded in the present moment. We'll learn to use bodily sensations and energy as one such anchor. To help emotional release, we'll try activities that get our energy moving, such as Body Tapping and breathing exercises. The practice part of this guide will show you exactly how to do this.

A range of tools can help you establish a solid anchor in your body, drawing your mind back whenever it tries to escape the present moment and your body. By maintaining this connection to your body, you'll navigate the healing journey more smoothly, staying centered through any turbulence on the path to emotional release.

Tackling old traumas and deeply held emotions through your body demands the gentleness of a healer's touch and the enduring strength of a warrior's determination. Instead of avoiding the challenging parts, it's important to go straight to the core of what your emotions are trying to tell you. Approach this process with genuine honesty and dedication, as it's a path to uncovering your true self beneath these layers of emotion.

Within each of us, two distinct versions of the self coexist. One seeks truth and connection, radiating with bright consciousness, confidence, and love. It is unafraid to risk everything for authenticity. The other finds comfort in the familiar, avoiding discomfort and fleeing from the unsettling depths of self-awareness.

You'll encounter both versions of yourself while releasing and healing suppressed emotions. Choose the one yearning for truth and freedom. The other version may ask, "Why reopen old wounds?" "What if I lose control?" Don't yield to this side. Instead, embrace your truth without hesitation. Allow everything inside you to surface, and let your truth come out. This path demands courage, vulnerability, honesty, and compassion but is also profoundly liberating and transformative.

Valerie's Story

Valerie is from First Mesa on the Hopi Nation, in the northeast corner of Arizona. During the COVID-19 pandemic, her community faced some devastating losses and, at that time, did not gather for their Hopi ceremonies due to the pandemic safety guidelines. Valerie looked for other ways of healing as her culture's traditional ceremonies were not available to her.

"We were barely recovering from someone passing, then someone else was dying, one after another," she recalls. Among those lost were key figures in her community, individuals essential for leading ceremonies and preserving tradition.

Among these losses, one hit Valerie particularly hard—the passing of one of the oldest members of her community, someone who was like a mother to her. This elder held a wealth of knowledge and was a source of comfort and wisdom throughout Valerie's life. However, her sudden departure left Valerie unable to say farewell or express her gratitude. "I got the news while I was driving down south with my kids," Valerie recounts. "The grief I felt that day was immense; I couldn't hold back the tears. I was crying so hard that I don't remember driving, and I had to stop myself because I didn't want to scare my kids or cause an accident."

Before attending the Love Heals Retreat, Valerie grappled with persistent stomach pain, which turned out to be caused by a cyst. A couple of years before, she'd had a cyst that grew abnormally large, and she'd had to have surgery to remove it. She was alarmed to learn she was developing another cyst. Her doctor suggested a biopsy to check for cancer. Alongside this concern, she endured severe pain in her right knee, hips, ankles, and feet.

"As we started tapping the stomach area and learned about keeping the belly warm, the Water Up, Fire Down energy principle, it clicked for me," she says. "I participated in all the sessions wholeheartedly." Through this practice, Valerie realized the deep-seated impact of the losses during the pandemic. "I was carrying this burden of emotions without knowing how to release them," she reflects. "As I relived those difficult memories and released my emotions, my pain got worse, and at some point, it felt unbearable. But deep down in my heart, I knew I needed this process. As I continued going through the tapping, vibration exercises, and energy meditations, I felt my body begin healing. Toward the end of the retreat, I realized that most of the pain had subsided." Valerie continued to use the techniques she learned at Sedona Mago daily to keep her body pain-free.

Valerie underwent her medical procedure a couple of weeks after returning home from the retreat. The news from the doctor astonished her: "The cyst has disappeared." She couldn't believe it. "Wait, did you just say the cyst went away?" she asked incredulously. "Yes, it's gone," her doctor confirmed. "Our bodies can heal themselves, and yours decided it wanted to heal itself."

"Through our emotions, we can keep the pain in our body," Valerie concludes. "You always hear it, you read it in books, people tell you not to stuff it down, but I never thought it could cause excruciating physical pain like that."

"I know I'm not alone in this struggle within our community. Many others silently suffer similar burdens," Valerie acknowledges. "I'm determined to make a difference in my life . . . I hope to open up opportunities for others to find the healing I've found with my Sedona Mago family."

Energy and Emotions

As you continue observing and releasing your emotions through energy practice, you'll gradually understand that all emotions are essentially the same. Initially, you might find this idea challenging to accept. After all, how can anger, happiness, joy, and fear be identical when they feel so different?

The word *emotion* comes from the Latin *emovere*, meaning to stir up or prompt a specific response. From an energetic perspective, emotions arise when external stimuli stir up your energy. Despite their individual characteristics, all emotions share a fundamental trait: they arise from stirred-up energy.

Consider how a single trigger can evoke diverse emotional responses depending on your energy level. When your energy is high, you might react angrily to unfair treatment, demanding a resolution. Yet, during moments of low energy, feelings of depression may overshadow anger, leading you to internalize the situation to avoid confrontation.

Emotions are reactions to what's happening around us, stirring our inner energy. When things settle and we have expressed these emotions properly, our energy returns to a harmonious, balanced state. But if we hold back our emotions or don't deal with them well, that stirred-up energy gets stuck inside us, creating a blockage. It doesn't matter if it's anger, sadness, or any other feeling—they all can be stored as stuck energy in our body.

So, no matter what emotion you're dealing with, the solution is similar from an energy standpoint. You need to find ways to activate your energy to release these blockages, allowing your energy to flow freely through your body again. I stress the importance of engaging in exercises that awaken and mobilize your energy for this reason.

Navigating Emotions

When releasing your emotions, the intention behind your actions is crucial. Approach this process aiming to connect with your true self, the core of who you are, beyond the fleeting nature of emotions. Without this focused intention, there's a risk of feeling overwhelmed, like drowning in a turbulent sea of feelings. To navigate these waters more smoothly, remember that the goal isn't to become consumed by the emotion but rather to navigate through it. Fully facing your feelings isn't about intensifying them; it's about moving through and releasing them to connect with your true self.

The path to emotional healing requires a delicate balance between fully experiencing our emotions and learning to view them with a sense of detachment. Understand that while our emotions are deeply felt experiences, they do not encompass all we are. By adopting the stance of the observer consciousness we discussed in Chapter 2, we can step back and witness our emotions as if from the outside. This doesn't mean dismissing them but rather acknowledging them without becoming consumed by them. It's similar to watching clouds pass in the sky: we see their shapes and feel their presence, but we know they are not the sky itself.

Grounding techniques such as tapping, deep breathing, and tuning into the subtle energy sensations within the body are essential during this process. These practices do more than facilitate the release of emotional energy; they also help cultivate a mindset focused on our deeper, authentic selves. By anchoring our attention in the body, we create a safe space for emotions to surface and be observed without judgment. It's a way of saying, "I see you, I honor you, but you do not control me."

Moreover, dedicating time to expanding our awareness of the energy within can greatly enhance our ability to observe emotions without becoming lost in them. This detached perspective isn't about disconnection but about fostering an understanding that we are more than our emotions. Through energy awareness practice, we train ourselves to witness emotions as they arise, feel them fully, and then release them gracefully without allowing them to define our identity or dictate our actions.

As we navigate this journey, the balance of acceptance and letting go becomes a dance of sorts—one where we learn the steps of honoring our emotions while also learning to release them with grace. This practice brings us closer to our true selves, the part of us that remains constant beneath the ebb and flow of emotional experiences. We come to see that our capacity for healing is as much about embracing our emotions as it is about knowing when and how to let them go, paving the way for a deeper, more authentic connection with ourselves.

Paige's Story

In Paige's third-grade year at a religious school, a day that began like any other took a heart-wrenching turn. As the lunch bell signaled the end of recess, Paige and her friend Chelsy followed their daily routine, heading toward the school's front doors to resume their afternoon classes. But an unexpected whim seized Chelsy, compelling her to suggest a detour to a side entrance. Little did they know that this spontaneous choice would lead to a heartbreaking accident.

The side entrance featured an old, weathered door, part glass and part wood, blending into the school's stone walls. Chelsy reached to push it open but found it wouldn't budge. Unknown to them, a boy on the other side was pushing against the bar. Paige stepped in to assist, pushing alongside Chelsy for a moment. However, as Paige stepped back, the built-up tension reached its limit, causing the glass to shatter.

Right then, a piece of glass flew straight and sharp, hitting Chelsy and injuring her badly, suggesting it might have cut an artery. Chelsy's screams pierced the air, as she stumbled down the steps. Paige watched, horrified, as Chelsy disappeared around the corner and vanished into the chaos of students drawn by the commotion.

Although it was a tragic accident for which Paige was not responsible, the memory was deeply embedded in her brain and body, and it tormented her throughout her life. Paige thought the broken glass shards got her friend because she stepped back at the right time.

Paige said, "I had felt that the wrong person might have died. If I had been the one that got cut, Chelsy would probably have been married, had kids, and become a grandma. Her life would have been more substantial than my life."

She suffered from low self-esteem and deep depression throughout her life. She took medication to treat the depression and had many therapy sessions, but she never fully dealt with the trauma from when she was eight years old. She says, "I shoved the emotions down, distracted myself from them, and just ignored them. Even when I talked to therapists, we didn't go deep into it because I wasn't ready and wasn't willing to do the work."

When she followed a meditation exercise looking back on her life, she reached her eighth year and thought, "I no longer want to carry this burden, and I am eager to release it. That was just an unfortunate, tragic accident. Now I'm ready to forgive myself, forgive Chelsy who left that day, and all things and people involved." She felt it was time to finally free herself from the guilt that had followed her for more than 50 years, and she was able to do that.

"I didn't have dreams and thought nothing more could be done for Paige. But now, knowing that I've had this breakthrough, I'm thinking that I could still create the life that I want. I'm 64 and may have another 20 or 30 years to live. I know I haven't reached my highest potential, and I know there's a better version of Paige that I want to have."

* * *

The narratives of Ericka, Valerie, and Paige offer a profound glimpse into how our emotional states significantly impact our physical health. These stories illustrate the physiological effects of suppressing emotions and the transformative power of facing and releasing them. Though often challenging, this journey reveals a universal truth: healing begins with courageously confronting our deepest fears, pains, and memories.

CHAPTER 7

RADIATING LOVE AND LIGHT WITHIN

Many of us carry the burden of past pains and disappointments, leading to a life lived behind closed doors of our own making. We learn to be cautious, often too cautious, due to experiences where trust led to hurt or betrayal. This fear of vulnerability prompts us to keep ourselves locked away, safe but isolated. We build walls and layers around our hearts, convincing ourselves that this is the way to self-protection.

In this state of self-imposed security, we often find ourselves trapped, unable to fully express who we are or fulfill our purpose. There's a constant internal dialogue driven by fear: "What if I open up and get hurt again? What if I'm taken advantage of?" This fear, deeply rooted in past experiences, dictates our actions and limits our ability to live freely and authentically.

Living in this protective bubble, we manage life within the confines of what we know, never venturing too far for fear of the unknown. While seeming safe, this cautious approach restricts us from experiencing life's fullness and prevents us from fully being our true selves. Then, our lives become filled with just managing the day-to-day status quo. We live each day just solving that day's problems without unlocking our true potential. This is how being stuck in life happens.

Living this way takes away our curiosity, excitement, and joy, making our lives feel stagnant. Each day becomes about mere survival, distancing us from the richness of life. We become disengaged, not just from the people around us, but also from ourselves, undermining our sense of self-worth and ability to love ourselves. We start to believe we have no love to give and further barricade our hearts.

Path to Open Yourself to Love

Many viewers of the *Love Heals* film found that one scene resonated deeply with them. In that scene, Rachel shared, "When Dr. Ericka told me on the first day, I want you to put your hand over your heart and say, 'I love myself,' I couldn't do it." This is not just Rachel's story but echoes a universal struggle for self-acceptance.

Biologist Bruce Lipton says when he asks his workshop audience to affirm, "I love myself," they laugh and comply. However, when he tests their belief using kinesiology, muscle testing reveals that 80–90 percent don't honestly believe it.

He suggests this is because we are often criticized in ways meant to motivate us, but these criticisms can lead us to think that we are not enough, that we are not deserving, lovable, or worthy. This belief is not a conscious thought but a subconscious program that plays out in the background, influencing our self-perception and actions. This belief system, rooted in criticism and negative reinforcement from childhood, dictates our feelings toward ourselves in adulthood, making self-love a challenging concept for many people.

Lipton also says that the function of the mind is to create coherence between our beliefs and our reality. If we have a program in our mind that tells us we are not lovable, then the function of the mind is to generate behavior that reveals that we are not lovable.

In other words, our mind tries to match our beliefs and actions. So, if we believe we are not lovable, our mind will make us act in ways that make this belief seem true. We might push people away or not notice when someone cares for us, making us feel unlovable, just like we believed. It's like our mind proves our belief is correct by influencing our behavior.

I resonate deeply with Dr. Lipton's observation that many people struggle with self-love. I've encountered numerous individuals who, despite achieving impressive social status and wealth, struggle with self-acceptance. No matter their accomplishments or possessions, they still struggle to accept themselves fully.

Following the Love Heals Retreat, Rachel shared a powerful realization: "Now I can say, 'I love me, and I deserve me. I deserve everything I want in this world. I know I am worthy, lovable, and amazing. The world benefits because I'm here.'" What sparked Rachel's transformation and the changes seen in many others throughout the film?

To understand this, let's take another look at the healing process we've talked about repeatedly, as it's critical to opening our hearts to love. I've brought this up in almost every chapter to ensure you understand its importance.

The initial step involves being fully present in your body, anchoring yourself in the now. Start activating your energy with practices like Body Tapping. This sensitizes your body, letting suppressed blockages rise to the surface. During this phase, you confront past pains, buried memories, and emotions that you've either repressed or were previously unaware of.

Through this process of being present, you realize that the barriers to your openness are not necessarily the environment, circumstances, or other people. It's a revelation that the closure is of your own making. You might have convinced yourself that you are safeguarded by not opening up, but now you start to see that the walls you built for protection were keeping you trapped. It becomes clear that you've been cutting yourself off from others and the world, making yourself stuck. This is when you understand that *you* have been the one stopping yourself from being accessible and able to love.

Once you acknowledge these self-imposed barriers, you face a critical decision. This is where the power of choice comes into play. Do you continue to live within the limitations you've created? Or do you opt for change and healing, freeing yourself to discover the true self beneath those layers and the boundless love and freedom that follow?

Choosing "Yes to Truth" over the familiar comfort of safety and security marks a significant breakthrough at this juncture. You arrive at your true self, the ultimate destination on your journey to healing.

The love discovered through meeting your true self is beyond tremendous; it's an expansive, boundless experience beyond expression through words. Those who have encountered it often share, "This must be what love feels like," "I've never felt this kind of love before," and "It was just pure, unconditional." Such expressions reflect the profound and transformative nature of this love. The most profound healing unfolds in these precious moments of embracing such love. Feeling it and immersing yourself in its essence leads to extraordinary transformation.

Pain psychologist Dr. Les Aria mentioned that the brain must feel safe for healing to occur. He believes love is a critical safety component, stating, "When you feel loved, whether it's from a spiritual perspective, a human being, a dog, or a community with whom you feel connected, that is safety."

When people experience the profound love that comes from meeting their true selves, they often simply say, "Everything's okay." This simple, reassuring phrase arises because true self-love eradicates all the fears we have created and provides a complete, unconditional sense of security. When we feel this secure, we are unafraid and unstoppable. It is the most profound sense of safety we can give ourselves and the most potent environment where healing occurs.

Often, we feel inadequate, believing we need something more to be complete. Our education and experiences have taught us that value comes from achieving something or behaving in specific ways. These ideas make us think we're worthless unless we meet specific goals, obtain certain items, or act a certain way. People dealing with substantial physical or emotional issues often tie their self-worth to overcoming these challenges. Consequently, they believe they will be finally worth something if they fix their problems or heal, making self-acceptance difficult.

The truth is, you're not lacking anything. You are already complete, absolutely precious, and valuable from the moment you were born into this world. You are already beautiful just as you are, without needing anything to validate your worth.

How can you truly understand your value? Is there a way to confirm it? You don't acquire this insight through traditional learning; it's something you recognize within yourself. You must return to yourself and sense your inherent preciousness and value. This awareness comes naturally when you connect with your true self through your senses and energy.

Meeting your true self changes your view on love. You realize that the love you've been trying to get, believing you were lacking, is already inside you. You're already full of love—you are love itself.

We often seek love outside ourselves, fearing we won't be loved or belong. But when you connect to your true self, you discover you're made of love. Love effortlessly flows within you, and it can be given freely without any conditions. This means we can share love freely because it comes from something bigger than us. When you grasp this big truth, you see you're not just looking for love—you're a never-ending source. After searching for love for so long, you realize you've been full of love. This understanding gives you a deep feeling of comfort, joy, and a connection you can't get from anyone else. You feel a love for yourself that's so strong it brings you to tears, filling your heart with warmth and healing.

Wendy's Story

Throughout her life, Wendy grappled with body image issues, heavily influenced by the words and expectations of society and the significant men in her life. She developed a belief that her value and acceptance depended on meeting specific physical standards. This constant pressure left Wendy feeling like she never fully measured up, leading to a long struggle with self-acceptance.

During the Love Heals Retreat, she was introduced to a particular exercise and meditation focused on her lower abdomen, a part of her body she had always struggled to accept. During this meditation, Wendy had a revelation: this very part of her body was the first home for her children. She reflected, "What an absolute miracle and honor of my life that my body was a first home for the five most beautiful humans on the planet."

This realization sparked a sense of awe and reverence for her body, something she had once viewed with disdain. Wendy was overwhelmed with love and gratitude for her body and, by extension, for herself. "The most profound takeaway from my time with the retreat is a deeper love of self that I've never experienced before," she shared.

For the first time in 45 years, Wendy could say, "I love myself," and truly feel it. She always thought that she was either not enough or too much. Whether it was about her appearance, spirituality, or kindness, Wendy always found herself lacking. On the other hand, her personality traits, such as being blunt, honest, or strong-willed, were also seen as too much. She took whatever people told her personally, and it became her insecurity and even led to self-hatred and self-loathing.

"There was a brick wall in front of me, and when I felt the indescribable love for myself, bricks were falling. Wendy, she's coming out and emerging, and I was getting glimpses of it. I found myself saying how amazing I am to be like this and what a gift I am. It was so beautiful. It's almost scary because I've never been this way in the world before. I think I'm just going to start crying because I don't have words for this," Wendy expressed.

Wendy has been dealing with knee pain for over 10 years and had a knee replacement surgery two years before the retreat, but recovery has been challenging. Letting out her emotions helped ease her knee pain.

Wendy shares her newfound insight: "This is the first time that I can remember not even thinking about my knee. I didn't even know I could heal to this level. I just thought I'm just going to have pain, and I have to square with that. Now I know I don't have to."

Love that Comes from Your True Self

When you connect with your true self, you discover genuine self-esteem and self-love. True self-esteem comes from valuing yourself, not through comparing or competing with others. It's not about only feeling valuable when others recognize you or feeling inferior because you believe someone else is superior in some way.

True self-esteem comes from knowing your true self, which is inherently wise, meaningful, and valuable. When you recognize this part of yourself, you naturally feel a strong sense of worth. Realizing that your true essence is resilient and untouchable by external harm helps you to love yourself deeply and without condition.

This kind of self-esteem isn't about how you stack up against others; it's a deep sense of self-worth that comes from within, no matter what. Relying on comparisons to feel good about yourself is risky—it can easily lead to feelings of inadequacy or even depression when someone new comes along, or it might make you feel falsely superior and dismissive of others. On the other hand, the self-respect and love that come from connecting with your true self provide a constant source of fulfillment and joy, no matter what's going on around you.

Each of us is unique, with no exact match out there. You are who you are, distinct and incomparable. When you discover your true self, you realize that loving yourself doesn't need conditions or reasons. You'll feel a sense of pride and love for simply being you. Despite your flaws and the challenges you face, you'll find ways to embrace and love yourself. Even when you're struggling with failure and fear, your love for yourself grows more intense. This self-love will become stronger and more passionate than any love you've extended to others.

You'll learn the difference between emotional love and true self-love on this journey. Emotional love, influenced by our ego and immediate feelings, changes continually based on our beliefs and our reactions to our surroundings. One day, it can be intensely passionate; the next, it might turn indifferent, fearful, envious, unkind, angry, or controlling. This form of love relies entirely on our own perceptions and the words, attitudes, beliefs, and actions of those around us, making it inherently unstable.

True self-love originates from our spiritual nature, embodying an absolute, unwavering, and ever-present essence, regardless of circumstances. This constant source of support guides us as we deepen our connection to it. It's a steadfast presence within us, even when it seems elusive. By embracing true self-love, we can accept and heal all aspects of ourselves. It allows us to move beyond past versions of ourselves that no longer serve us toward new versions that genuinely reflect our essence.

Our Capacity to Love

Many of us feel like we're running out of love to give, especially when we keep showing love to those around us without it being returned, making us feel drained and as if our reservoir of love has run dry. Yet, the truth is that we all have a limitless capacity to love that doesn't fade away. We're equipped to wholeheartedly embrace life, love ourselves, and love everything in our world. Recognizing this can transform our focus from merely trying to protect ourselves to actively pursuing healing and personal growth.

During this journey, many learn to forgive and let go, breaking free from the hold of emotional turmoil and deep-seated grudges. Rather than dwelling on old wounds, you begin to view yourself and others through a lens that reflects your true self. You realize the importance of forgiving your mistakes and breaking the self-imposed limits that have held you back. It's about allowing yourself to move past moments of self-rejection or self-loathing.

Forgiveness is also usually the key to finally releasing pent-up emotions, especially when holding on to something from our past. While our current situations can be changed, and we can build better futures for ourselves, nothing can be changed about what has occurred in the past. While we may be able to seek some sort of justice for what has happened, ultimately, the past is immovable and unchangeable. You can only change your reaction and relationship with what has happened.

However, I understand entirely how difficult it can be to let go of that which has caused deep mental and emotional trauma. Humans can do terrible things to each other, and the harm can shake our perceptions of ourselves and the world around us. But, if we do not let go and forgive, we relive the worst moments of our lives in perpetuity. When we forgive, we finally let the past stay in the past instead of allowing it to affect the present.

We learned the first energy principle: "Energy follows where the mind goes." Thus, when we hold sadness or resentment about an event, constantly replaying the story in our mind, we bring more and more energy to that memory. In the body, this may result in a buildup of tension and stagnant energy, which blocks the flow of energy in the energy pathways, causing pain and stiffness in those areas. The body is very good at restoring the Water Up, Fire Down energy balance but cannot do so until these blockages are released.

Love is indeed at the center of forgiveness. Forgiveness means returning to a proper state of energy flow in relationship to other people, the universe, and ourselves. This means loving ourselves, loving others, and loving all that is, even the difficult things. On the energetic level, love is merely the free flow of energy between elements in our lives—between myself and my soul, between myself and others, and between myself and the universe.

Our egoic senses wrongly tell us that we are separate from others, but we are not. Through energy, we are connected to everyone and everything. We cut off energy from ourselves and the other person when we attempt to cut off from or reject anything because of our judgments and resentments. Thus, when we forgive, we reestablish energy flow, and true healing can begin.

According to Fred Luskin, PhD, Director of the Stanford University Forgiveness Projects and author of *Forgive for Good*, forgiveness is a process of letting go. It involves releasing the ways we've bound ourselves in suffering by arguing with the unfolding of our own lives. It doesn't come easy, and it takes courage to understand that we were once confronted with something outside of our ability to cope. As Luskin says, "It's like, yes, of course it happened to me. And yes, of course, I was a victim for a while. But now, that's not what I want to be. That's its power."

In this space of forgiveness, you learn to extend love to those who have wronged you or caused you pain, even if they don't acknowledge their actions or apologize. You discover that your ability to love is limitless and isn't diminished by others' actions. You understand that the one who suffered the most from clinging to past resentments was yourself. By cultivating deep compassion, love, and trust in yourself, you manage to release these burdens. This leads to a profound feeling of freedom, peace, and liberation.

As you connect with this infinite source of love, you find that sharing love becomes effortless and deeply fulfilling. The more love you share, the stronger your capacity to love grows. With this mindset, you begin to perceive others in a new light. Recognizing that we all share the same source of love, you see reflections of this love in everyone you meet. This universal connection opens you to new possibilities of understanding and empathy, breaking down barriers and preconceptions.

Connecting to the Divine

The moment you connect with your true self, you feel your heart begin to overflow with love, and a vibrant energy courses through your body. This energy can either surge through you like a mighty storm or embrace you as gently as soft cotton. It's often accompanied by a sensation of openness, expansion, and a profound sense of connection, alongside deep feelings of love and freedom. Many find this energy provides support and guidance. When we peel back the layers of thoughts and emotions, at our core, we discover our true self, connected to a vast source of energy and consciousness. This connection is what some people refer to as divinity. I would describes it as "universal energy and consciousness."

The concept of divinity, as discussed here, transcends personal religious or spiritual beliefs. It is suggested as a universal force that permeates everything in the world, including each of us. This sacred presence is not remote or separate from us; it is an integral part of our essence. The process of connecting with the divine within doesn't necessarily rely on specific spiritual or religious practices; it's more about recognizing and nurturing the divine spark that resides in each of us. We are more than just our physical bodies or our thoughts.

Deep down, there's a universal longing to feel connected to something much greater than ourselves.

Divinity can be likened to a vast ocean—a metaphor for a spiritual force or energy that fills the universe with qualities such as love, wisdom, and creativity. Our true selves are compared to the waves on this ocean; each wave is distinct and temporary, yet made of the same water as the ocean itself. Despite our unique personalities and life experiences, we are all intrinsically connected to this divine ocean. Waves may appear separate on the surface, but they are always a part of the ocean, inseparable from it. In this sense, the ocean expresses itself through these very waves. Regardless of how differently we experience or express this divinity, the notion is that we're all part of the same spiritual essence.

Thus, when we discover our true self, we connect with the divine essence that fills the universe. Experiencing love within ourselves is a way to tap into the universe's endless love. We come into this world equipped with all we need to uncover our true selves. Within each of us lies a spark of divinity, bright and complete. Finding our true selves ignites this spark, allowing divine energy to flow into us and enrich our lives.

To engage with this divine energy, I suggest that we practice three things: opening up, receiving, and letting it flow freely. This connection to divine energy is unconditional. By simply opening ourselves up and being ready to receive that energy, we invite it into our lives. All it takes is a genuine desire to connect with that energy and open our hearts to it. Once received, we let this energy move through us, circulating within and extending out into the world. Like nature, which exists in a constant state of flow and renewal, we too can embrace this principle. By sharing the vast love and energy we receive, we enrich ourselves and the world around us. The unconditional love we experience by connecting with this divine energy has the power to heal and restore everything. The love that healed us now flows from us into the world, and the cycle of healing continues.

Leah's Story

Growing up in a very conservative religious family, Leah was taught from an early age to follow a strict standard of morality and to judge others through that lens. Anything that didn't align with this belief system should be rejected, even if it was a part of her identity.

As a child, Leah would have moments when she felt she was connecting directly with God. These moments were precious to her. Yet, most of the time, fear overshadowed this spiritual connection, fear that God would be furious about any misstep. It felt like a burden as she carried the negative energy of judging herself against the moral standards she was raised to believe were necessary for a relationship with God.

When Leah's best friend came out as gay in high school, she didn't know how to react. Her upbringing screamed that being gay was wrong, so she froze and walked away, destroying a friendship that meant the world to her. Later, Leah came to realize she was gay as well, adding another layer of complexity to her internal battle with her beliefs and self-acceptance.

Taught her whole life that she was wrong for things as simple as wearing a hat during a worship service or not dressing as expected of girls, the weight of constant judgment and her fear of rejection caused her great suffering. The weight of the negative energy she had carried her whole life, viewed through a conservative religious lens, led her to believe she was fundamentally flawed. "I felt I was the worst," she recalls.

People would proclaim their love for her, but it always came with an "if you . . ." or a "but" attached. It felt like the acceptance was never genuine, always conditional, and the rejection cut deep for Leah. The standards others expected of her were impossible to meet because they did not reflect what she truly wanted to be. She couldn't live a life trying to meet others' expectations, which she mistakenly believed were also God's expectations.

About two years ago, Leah realized that the beliefs she grew up with no longer resonated. Since then, she has been exploring what felt good for her spiritually, but she often felt lost and empty. She craved the spiritual connection she once had but didn't know where to find it.

During the Love Heals Retreat, it dawned on Leah how many things she was still clinging to from long ago. "I thought I had left it all behind, but it still weighed me down. I still had this judgmental belief in myself because I had been conditioned to feel that way ever since I was a kid." She began to understand that she first needed to release the negative energy she had been carrying for her spiritual growth.

When she was guided to feel the divine energy, Leah mustered the courage to let go of those old beliefs about herself. She was able to release the burden of guilt, shame, and nonacceptance, processing these heavy emotions that were no longer serving her. The divine energy felt like coming home. It was an overwhelming sense of love and acceptance, pure and embracing, precisely what she'd been searching for.

But it was new and scary because Leah had always feared being herself, and she had been raised to believe that not fitting into the box meant judgment or even damnation. She began to understand that within the embrace of divine energy, she didn't have to live like that anymore. She realized that living up to others' expectations was impossible if it meant not being true to herself.

This experience helped her release the punitive image of God she had been holding on to and embrace a new understanding of the divine as something intimately connected to and part of herself. She finally understood that embracing her true self was the key to living as the beautiful person God created.

"I didn't receive the acceptance that I craved ever since I was a kid from my spiritual upbringing, but now I can give that acceptance to myself," Leah reflected. Now, she knows there's nothing inherently wrong with her. "I know I'm worthy, and love and accept myself just as I am." She's on a journey to being herself, aware of the challenges ahead but equipped with the tools to navigate them.

Love Heals Practice Guide

The stories of Wendy's awakening and Leah's acceptance of her true self illuminate a path from self-imposed limitations to a place of boundless love and acceptance. This journey, which includes profound self-discovery and connection with the divine, reveals a fundamental truth: we are not simply seekers of love; we are its source.

Accepting this truth invites us to tear down the walls we have built around our hearts, to look beyond the fears and scars of our past, and to step into the light of our true selves. The love we have always sought has always been within us, waiting to be acknowledged, nurtured, and shared. This love, which is infinite and unconditional, is our birthright and our most potent source of strength and healing.

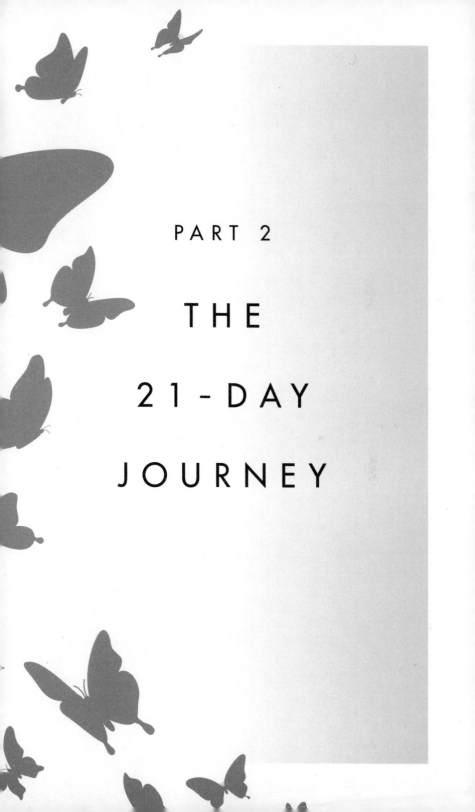

PART 2

THE
21-DAY
JOURNEY

CHAPTER 8

PREPARING YOURSELF FOR THE JOURNEY

So far, we've explored the fundamental principles that foster true healing. Through real people's stories, we've seen individuals overcome physical pain and emotional trauma, finding genuine self-acceptance. I sincerely hope these experiences resonate with you deeply, sparking a desire for change, growth, and healing in your own life.

The *Love Heals Practice Guide* isn't just for reading; it's for action. Now, let's dive into the heart of this journey. Over the next 21 days, you'll engage in daily exercises and meditations central to this practice. While 21 days may feel like both a marathon and a sprint, it's ample time for you to notice tangible shifts in both body and mind. With steadfast commitment, I believe you'll feel the healing power of this process taking root within you.

These practices aren't just abstract ideas—they're the very ones that real people like you embraced at the Love Heals Retreat featured in the film. Through these practices, Valerie healed her cyst, Wendy found relief from a decade of chronic knee pain, and Dana experienced tangible reductions in her back and leg pain. Paige, after 50 years, finally released the burden of survivor's guilt, while Rachel discovered profound self-love and acceptance.

Over the last four decades, millions worldwide have embraced these practices and experienced the healing power of the mind-body connection and genuine self-love. Welcome to a journey of authenticity, where growth, healing, and true self-discovery unfold in real, tangible ways.

Guidelines to Keep in Mind

This three-week practice is based on Brain Education and its energy principles and mirrors the structure of the Love Heals Retreat I lead.

You'll dive into exercises to awaken your physical senses and strengthen your core in the first week. As you engage in these practices, you'll feel more grounded, experience heightened vitality, and cultivate greater resilience.

Moving into the second week, you'll focus on the patterns of your emotions, thoughts, and habits. You'll confront the underlying issues holding you back by staying connected to your body and awakening your energy senses. By releasing what no longer serves you, you'll feel a profound shift in your emotional well-being, paving the way for greater heart power.

Finally, in the third week, you'll explore the depths of your spiritual essence. Through practices that tap into your brain's limitless potential, you'll experience moments of insight, creativity, and connection to something greater than yourself. These experiences will guide you toward a deeper understanding of your purpose and potential.

Energy is the thread weaving through this 21-day healing journey, connecting your body, mind, and soul. You'll initiate genuine healing and true self-love and acceptance by tuning into and expanding this energy.

This practice is open to everyone, whether you're new to mind-body practices or have years of experience. Regardless of your spiritual or religious background, I invite you to approach it with an open mind and discover what resonates with you.

Here are some practical guidelines to remember to get the most out of your 21-day journey:

1. The 21-day practice is laid out in a step-by-step sequence, intentionally structured progressively to unlock your energy and foster healing. Start by sticking to the prescribed order for the first 21 days, experiencing each step as it comes. After three weeks, you're encouraged to personalize your approach, picking and mixing techniques that best fit your needs and preferences. This way, you can keep what works for you and adapt your practice for long-term benefits.

2. Commit to performing the exercises outlined here daily for 21 days, allocating roughly 30–40 minutes for each session. If your schedule

permits, aim for twice daily sessions, once in the morning and again in the evening, to amplify the benefits. On days when you have more flexibility, like weekends, extending your practice time can substantially enhance the healing effects that you experience.

3. Maintain a practice journal. Document your journey of awakening and note the physical and mental transformations you observe as you engage with the practice. Journaling is a potent tool for healing. It bolsters your self-awareness, offering a mirror to reflect on your inner state. It aids in untangling your thoughts, providing clarity, and facilitating a healthy release of emotions. Additionally, it serves as a motivational reminder of how far you've come, reinforcing your commitment to your growth journey.

4. I've provided a few journal prompts to guide your reflections after your daily practice sessions. However, these are just starting points. The key is to authentically record your journey of transformation and awakening every day in a way that resonates with you. Your journal is a space for recording your authentic experiences, thoughts, and discoveries.

5. Welcome the discomfort, pain, boredom, and challenges you experience during your practice. These experiences aren't obstacles to sidestep but valuable signals pointing you toward areas of

your life needing attention and care. They catalyze healing and growth, revealing hidden layers of your being previously unnoticed. By confronting these feelings head-on, you uncover deeper parts of yourself.

6. Be honest and open with yourself. Let any feelings, thoughts, or sensations during your practice be fully felt and acknowledged rather than ignored or hidden. Being true to yourself is crucial to healing. When you listen and accept what's inside you, healing naturally follows. It starts with being honest with yourself and seeing and embracing everything you experience.

7. Prioritize yourself. It's common to dedicate a lot of time and effort to looking after others, sometimes at the expense of our self-care. For the next 21 days, make a conscious effort to carve out uninterrupted time for yourself. Switch off your phone, let your loved ones know you need this space undisturbed, and channel all your attention inward. This is your time to give yourself the care, focus, and nurturing you deserve. Treat each moment as a precious opportunity to reconnect with and tend to your own needs and well-being.

Willingness Is the Key

Through guiding many on their healing paths, I've seen firsthand how a person's willingness dramatically influences their healing. Almost everyone at the Love Heals Retreat finds great mind and body healing. Yet, those with a strong determination to heal witness truly remarkable transformations.

A true healing journey demands a willingness to face and work through deep issues, to look inward with honesty, and to open yourself up to vulnerability. It's natural to want to escape when facing physical discomfort and emotional pain, but remember, confronting these challenges with the perspective of an observer consciousness is central to healing.

This journey might seem dull at first, and you may easily get bored if you're not entirely focused. This happens because the exercises are indeed straightforward and tend to be repeated. However, if you wholeheartedly commit to the process, you'll find the experience fascinating and enlightening. You'll start noticing sensations in your body you might never have felt before and gain insights about yourself that were previously hidden.

The practices are here to guide you, but your healing depends on your dedication, your energy, and your willingness to embrace change. As you begin, do so with an open heart and a curious mind, ready to be amazed by your resilience and your heart's vast healing capacity.

CHAPTER 9

WEEK 1
AWAKENING
YOUR BODY

Your body is inherently wise and constantly works toward restoring your health. Retaining your ability to feel, connect with, and communicate with your body will guide you in understanding what you need to do to facilitate your healing.

In the first week, you'll work on reconnecting with your body's senses and feeling more grounded. Being grounded means your mind stays focused on what's happening in your body, noticing how you feel physically. Often, you may feel disconnected, like your thoughts are racing ahead and your body can't keep up, or as if your mind and body aren't working together. Your mind might be elsewhere, not paying attention to your body's feelings.

In the first week's exercises, you'll work on aligning your mind and body, helping you to concentrate on the present moment and become more aware of your bodily sensations. You'll learn to stay focused on the here and now, which helps you avoid getting overwhelmed by situations or reacting impulsively. This practice will enhance your awareness and strengthen your ability to handle stress, boosting your mental and physical resilience.

This process energizes the lower abdomen, central to your body's energy system. You will directly engage with the Water Up, Fire Down principle we discussed earlier, experiencing firsthand a cool head and warm lower abdomen. The first week's exercises aim to rebalance your energy, enhance physical vitality, foster an open heart, and clarify your mind.

1 Set Your Intention

On the first day, you'll dedicate time to understanding your current stage in the healing journey and your specific goals. This is also an opportunity to motivate yourself as you embark on the 21-day practice. You will engage in self-reflection, meditation, and journaling to facilitate this.

We have the power to shape our paths in life. By looking back and reflecting on ourselves, we open the door to dream and choose who we aspire to be. These choices have the transformative power to redefine us and steer our destiny in new directions. I believe this very power has guided you to this book.

If you've tried to heal and change repeatedly without feeling like you've made progress, it's natural to hesitate before giving it another shot. In these moments of hesitation, simplify your approach. Clear away distractions and concentrate solely on your longing for healing and transformation. Summon your courage and affirm to yourself, "Even so, I am ready to try again."

Your past experiences, whether they happened years ago or just moments ago, don't define you. What matters is your current, earnest desire for change and healing. Listen to that desire resonating within your heart. Let it guide you as you embark on this 21-day journey to your transformation.

Meditation: Self-Reflection

Find a comfortable position, sitting on the floor or in a chair. If you're sitting in a chair, keep your feet flat on the floor. Gently sway your upper body from side to side. Allow your neck, shoulders, and spine to relax and shake gently, moving your upper body quickly like a tree branch dancing in the breeze.

Inhale deeply and lift your shoulders toward your ears. As you exhale, let your shoulders drop and relax. Continue this movement of lifting and releasing your shoulders with your breath, repeating two or three more times.

Place your hands on your knees with your palms facing up, resting comfortably. Straighten your back and gently close your eyes. Turn your attention to your breath. Instead of trying to control it, simply let yourself breathe naturally and comfortably. Keep breathing in this relaxed way.

Turn your attention to your chest and feel it relax as you breathe deeply. Now, ask yourself: What changes do I want to see in my life? What am I searching for? Are there any pressing questions I'm struggling with? Take a moment to reflect on these questions, focusing quietly on the feelings and responses that arise within your heart. Trust that your heart holds the guidance you need.

As you focus on your chest, you might sense various thoughts or emotions beginning to surface. Let these feelings and thoughts come naturally without trying to stop or cling to them. Allow yourself to experience whatever rises from your heart without sorting or judging. Simply experience these sensations and emotions as they come and go.

You're deeply committed to finding healing and are ready for change in this very moment. A profound desire to reconnect with your true self is stirring within you. Now, more than ever, you're prepared to hear the voice of your soul.

Let the longing for change that resides in your heart envelop you fully. Allow this desire to permeate your heart and spread throughout your body and mind, infusing every cell of your being with its power.

Make a genuine promise to yourself. Promise to dedicate yourself to giving the best care and focus you can muster during this 21-day practice. Feel the sincerity of this commitment resonate deeply within your heart.

Conclude the meditation by taking a few deep breaths.

JOURNAL PROMPTS

1. What have you been searching for?
2. What actions have you taken to pursue what you believed you were seeking?
3. What are your goals for this 21-day journey?

2 Awaken Your Body's Senses

Today, you'll dive into the practical experience of awakening your body's senses with a straightforward activity: shaking. This exercise is accessible to everyone, no matter your level of physical fitness. By gently shaking your body, you'll introduce soothing vibrations that can rejuvenate and energize you from head to toe.

A key aspect of the energy practice you'll undertake is repeating simple movements. These movements might seem too easy at first glance, making you doubt their effectiveness as exercise. However, once you try them yourself, you'll be surprised by their powerful impact. The sensation is unexpectedly satisfying and invigorating.

These movements are more like a natural physiological response to restore bodily harmony and balance than ordinary exercises. Just as you yawn when sleepy or sigh when frustrated, shaking is a natural way for the body to release blocked energy.

When engaging in any exercises listed in this book, keep your attention focused on your breath and the body part you're working on. During the shaking exercise, you'll discover a deeper sense of release by paying particular attention to your exhale.

Exercise: Whole Body Shaking

You can perform this exercise with or without music. If you prefer using music, opt for tracks with repetitive drumbeats.

Begin by standing comfortably with your feet shoulder-width apart, ensuring they are firmly planted on the ground. Bend your knees slightly and initiate a gentle bouncing movement. Imagine a spring connecting your knees and ankles aiding this bounce, keeping your feet flat while your body experiences vibrations.

As you continue bouncing your knees, bring your awareness to different parts of your body, initiating vibrations within each area. Let the movement be fluid as you bounce and shake. Exhale audibly to deepen the effect throughout the session.

Gradually let the vibrations build, intensifying from your knees upward through your thighs and into your hips. As the vibrations reach your hips, begin to loosen your spine, imagining it waving like a snake

WATCH A VIDEO

from your tailbone through your lower, middle, and upper back. When the vibrations extend to your shoulders, allow them to start shaking naturally, extending the movement down through your arms to your fingertips to release tension.

Shift your focus to your neck, shaking your head gently from side to side, releasing any tension in your neck and head. Let the vibrations envelop your whole body while your feet remain planted and your body relaxes. Adjust your movements as needed to focus on any areas of stiffness or tension.

If you notice specific areas of tension, concentrate your shaking there, intensifying your movements and imagining the release of all heavy, stressful energies with each exhale. Let your body guide you, and trust in its natural movements.

Gradually stop shaking after you bring awareness to each part of your body. Depending on how much time you spend on each area, you can perform this exercise for 3–10 minutes.

Close your eyes, focus on your breath, and tune into the sensations in your body for 1–2 minutes. Notice any warm or tingling sensations, as they are signs of energy flowing within you. You are awakening your body's senses and tapping into your innate healing power.

Conclude the exercise with a few deep breaths.

JOURNAL PROMPTS

1. List all the sensations you felt during the exercise.
2. Identify any parts of your body that felt stiffer or more uncomfortable while shaking.
3. Describe the sensations you experienced during the breathing exercise after shaking.

DAY 3 Be in the Present Moment

Your healing and awakening are unfolding in this moment. The only time you can genuinely make an impact is now. Therefore, it's crucial to center your focus on the present moment, neither dwelling on the past nor drifting toward the future. Embrace the power of now, as it's a time you've never experienced. Each moment is new, and nothing can be exactly replicated. To heal, you must embrace the newness of this moment. Concentrate on what you feel now, what actions you can take, and release the rest.

Today, the focus is on grounding your mind in your body and nurturing awareness of the present moment through Whole Body Tapping. This technique involves tapping across your entire body with the palm or fist to awaken sensation and promote energy flow.

When I introduced this technique, many asked how it differs from the well-known Emotional Freedom Technique (EFT). EFT involves tapping specific points on your hands, face, or body with your fingers while focusing on the issue or feeling you want to address. It's known for its ability to improve mental health by helping with stress, anxiety, and fear.

EFT and Body Tapping both utilize energy principles but differ in their approach. While EFT aims to stimulate specific points, Body Tapping focuses on awakening sensations throughout the body. With Body Tapping, you tap a general area rather than pinpointing precise points. The goal is to improve the body's overall energy balance. Unlike EFT, where tapping is gentle, Body Tapping requires firmer tapping to generate stronger sensations. You focus on the impact you feel when your hand touches your body, the vibration it generates, and the various sensory experiences it triggers throughout your body.

During this exercise, concentrate on the specific part of the body you're tapping, and pay close attention to your exhaling breath. The goal is to truly *feel* your body. You'll gradually awaken previously unnoticed sensations through consistent practice, guided by your body's inherent wisdom. This process will deepen your understanding of your body, offering new insights for healing.

If tapping brings about more pain or discomfort, it indicates blocked energy that needs extra attention. Spend additional time tapping these areas to release the tension and promote healing.

Exercise: Whole Body Tapping

Stand with your legs shoulder-width apart. Begin by tapping the top of your head with your fingertips, keeping your wrist relaxed and employing a gentle snapping motion. Imagine the tapping penetrating your skull, rejuvenating your brain.

With each exhale, release tension, making a soft "whoo" sound. Progress from the upper to the lower back of the head and the base of the skull, tapping gently but firmly.

Continue to the sides of the head and behind the ears, spending extra time on any painful areas with deeper breaths. Move to tap the forehead and temples, visualizing stagnant energy leaving your brain, replaced by fresh oxygen and energy.

Extend your left arm comfortably in front of your body, palm facing up. Tap with the palm of your right hand from your left shoulder down to your left palm while bouncing your knees as you did during yesterday's Whole Body Shaking exercise. Switch hands and repeat the tapping motion from your right shoulder to your palm. Continue to focus on your exhalations and observe any sensations in your body.

WATCH A VIDEO

Next, tap your chest with both palms, then move to the left, abdomen, and right flank. Bend slightly at the waist and tap your lower back with both hands.

Bend your upper body, slightly widen your stance, and tap down the back of your thighs, calves, and ankles. Move from the ankles along the front of your legs, through the thighs, to the side of the groin. Tap along the outside of the thighs from the hip joint to the ankles. Tap from the ankles up to the inside of the groin area along the thighs.

Wherever you feel discomfort or the need to tap, continue tapping while breathing deeply. You can tap longer in areas that feel good to you, too. This exercise can take 3–10 minutes, depending on how much you tap each area.

When you're ready, return to your normal breathing and stop tapping.

Close your eyes and focus on the sensations in your body, breathing comfortably for about 1–2 minutes. Notice any tingling sensations, changes in temperature, or feelings of expansion and contraction. Feel grateful for the grounding sensation in your body and breath. Observe your mind becoming calmer and your breath naturally deepening.

Finish the exercise after taking a few deep breaths.

JOURNAL PROMPTS

1. Which part of your body felt uncomfortable when tapping?
2. Did you find it easy to concentrate during tapping, or was it a struggle?
3. What specific changes did you observe or experience as a result of the practice?

4 Appreciate Your Body

I view the body as the soul's sanctuary, a sacred vessel deserving our respect and care. Just as we honor temples for their spiritual significance, we should hold our bodies in the same regard.

However, often, we neglect our bodies, are overwhelmed by stress and discomfort, and seek escape from our physical and emotional burdens. Nurturing a positive relationship with our bodies is the foundation of our healing journey.

Today, you'll revisit Whole Body Tapping, followed by Body Appreciation Meditation. Your body is your eternal companion on the journey of healing and growth. Connecting deeply with your body fosters gratitude for its unwavering support through life's ups and downs. This gratitude nurtures your desire to care for your body and helps you discern its actual needs rather than operating on autopilot.

Meditation: Body Appreciation

Begin by performing the Whole Body Tapping exercise you did yesterday. Tap your entire body from head to toe, increasing the intensity slightly from yesterday. Spend extra time tapping on areas where you feel discomfort or pain. Focus on each part of your body as you tap, exhaling audibly to release tension. Aim to tap for about 10 minutes to awaken your body's senses fully.

After completing Whole Body Tapping, find a comfortable position on a chair or floor. Straighten your spine and relax your neck, shoulders, and arms. Place your hands on your knees with palms facing up. Close your eyes and direct your gaze downward. Breathe gently through your slightly open mouth and close it when breathing feels more comfortable.

With one hand on your chest and the other on your abdomen, feel the warmth and subtle movement under your hands as you breathe. Notice the gentle rise and fall of your chest and abdomen, allowing your breath to connect you with your body's rhythm.

From this place of physical connection, express gratitude sincerely, not just as a mental exercise but as a deeply felt appreciation for the life force pulsating within your body. Acknowledge any areas of stagnation, discomfort, or pain, and thank your body for being with you in this moment. Be grateful for the strength and resilience your body shows every day no matter your current state.

If you identify areas of discomfort, gently place your hand on them. If these areas are hard to reach, put your hand in a corresponding location on the front of your body. This physical touch can enhance your sense of connection and healing. Express your intention for healing and gratitude, silently or aloud.

Affirm your commitment to carry this sense of connection, gratitude, and awareness into your daily life.

Thank your body and yourself again for dedicating this time to self-awareness.

Conclude your meditation with a few deep breaths.

JOURNAL PROMPTS

1. Reflect on any differences you felt during today's tapping compared to yesterday's.
2. If a specific area of your body demanded your attention during the Body Appreciation Meditation, where was it, and what sensations did you experience there?
3. Write a letter to your body starting with "Dear body," expressing any thoughts or feelings that come to mind and sharing what you want to convey to your body.

Today, you're diving into a unique healing practice called Toe Tapping. Unlike Whole Body Tapping, where you use your hands to tap across your entire body, Toe Tapping involves the rhythmic tapping of the toes against each other. Although the movements vary, both practices aim to awaken the body's senses and stimulate its energy. Toe Tapping is particularly effective for restoring Water Up, Fire Down energy balance, as it helps redirect energy that typically rises to your head back down to your lower body and toes.

Breathing happens independently, like our heartbeat and blood pressure, without us thinking about it. However, breathing is unique because we can control it to some extent, and this attribute makes breathing a powerful healing tool. You can reduce stress by consciously slowing and deepening your breath, creating a feeling of ease and calm. After Toe Tapping, you'll focus on your breath, deeply connecting with the vital energy.

Exercise: Toe Tapping

You can do this exercise seated for convenience, but for deeper relaxation, consider lying down. Find a comfortable place to lie on your back and close your eyes. Bring your legs together, and extend your arms slightly away from your body, palms facing upward.

With your heels together, gently tap your feet together repeatedly, mimicking the motion of a windshield wiper, while focusing on your toes. Visualize energy sinking into your toes with each tap as energy follows where your mind goes.

As you continue, exhale through your mouth to release any stagnant energy, envisioning it leaving your body like stale air being expelled from a room with a fan.

After completing approximately 100 toe taps, take a brief one-minute rest. During this time, concentrate on your breath, and visualize any remaining stagnant energy leaving through your toes.

Repeat this for five sets of 100 toe taps, visualizing the release of energy from higher up in your body with each set. For example, when you do the second set, imagine stagnant energy leaving from your thighs and hips through your toes; for the third, from your lower back and abdomen; for the fourth, from your chest; and for the fifth, from your head and entire body. Remember to take a one-minute break after each set, focusing on your breathing and visualizing the release of stagnant energy.

After completing five sets of Toe Tapping, shift your focus inward, centering your awareness on your body as you breathe deeply. Feel the heaviness dissipating through your toes, replaced by a sense of lightness washing over you. Visualize this energy clearing from your head down to your chest, abdomen, and legs, exiting through the tips of your toes.

Notice the rhythm of your breath. See how it becomes effortlessly comfortable and deep. Sense this revitalized energy flowing within you, linking you to the essence of life. Your breath flows naturally, effortlessly sustaining your existence. Welcome this connection with your body, acknowledging it as an expression of life in the now.

Conclude the exercise with a few deep breaths.

JOURNAL PROMPTS

1. What sensations did you notice during Toe Tapping?
2. How did you feel when you focused on your breath afterward?
3. Did you have any meaningful awakenings or realizations today?

6 Let Your Pain Guide You

Self-awareness is essential for healing, as it offers insight into our thoughts, feelings, and actions. It acts like a flashlight in a dark room, revealing things previously unseen. By shining this light on ourselves, we can identify the sources of our pain or discomfort. This insight is crucial for healing, as recognizing the problem is the first step toward taking healing actions.

Yet, our self-awareness can diminish as we become disconnected from our body and mind. Developing it requires focus and, most importantly, honesty. Deep, honest self-observation is critical to understanding ourselves. This involves looking beneath our actions and emotions to find our needs and motivations. It's important to proactively engage with and understand the emotions, beliefs, habits, and behaviors that impede our healing and growth rather than avoiding or dismissing them.

Today, you'll engage in Abdominal Tapping, a practice central to your 21-day journey. This practice strengthens the connection between your body and mind, fostering Water Up, Fire Down energy balance. It helps you stay present, release stagnant energy, and embrace fresh energy that facilitates a deeper awakening.

While tapping, notice any discomfort or imbalance in your body or mind. Instead of seeking instant relief or solutions, continue tapping with kindness and compassion.

Pay attention to every sensation, thought, and emotion that arises, embracing them with detached observation.

If at any point your mind wanders and you start to complain about your pain, discomfort, or even boredom, bring your awareness to the sensation of your hands tapping your body and the vibrations it creates.

Notice any thoughts or feelings that arise and consciously release them with each exhale. If specific thoughts or emotions continue to emerge during your tapping, affirm to yourself, "My body is not me, but mine. My pain is not me, but mine. My emotions are not me, but mine." Vocalizing these affirmations can enhance their impact.

Exercise: Abdominal Tapping

Start by engaging in Whole Body Tapping while standing. Follow the sequence you learned on the third day, focusing extra time on areas where you feel pain or discomfort. As you tap, visualize the impact extending beyond your skin, reaching deep into your body. Keep your attention on the vibrations and sensations generated by your tapping.

As you tap your body, you might discover sore or uncomfortable spots. Sometimes, you might tap one place, like your right arm, but feel discomfort somewhere else, like your stomach or back. This is normal because all body parts are linked through nerves, connective tissues, and energy pathways. Don't try to ignore these feelings. Instead, accept them. Remember to breathe in

Love Heals Practice Guide

through your nose and out through your mouth while you're tapping. Aim to continue tapping your entire body for about 10 minutes.

Now, transition to Abdominal Tapping. You may typically use open palms or lightly clenched fists, but for today, opt for fists. Gently yet firmly tap just below your navel, alternating between your left and right fist. Ensure you apply enough intensity to stimulate the lower abdomen effectively. Maintain your focus with a steady, rhythmic tapping motion throughout the session.

WATCH A VIDEO

While tapping your lower abdomen, bounce your knees like in Whole Body Shaking. This movement boosts vibrations in your body, increasing the effectiveness of the tapping. Staying too stiff can tire you out quickly. Keep your upper body relaxed during tapping to prevent tension in your shoulders and arms. Exhale stagnant energy through your mouth.

Simply notice any sensations, thoughts, or feelings in your body and mind. You might experience pain, discomfort, or all sorts of distracting thoughts. Let these feelings and thoughts surface without clinging to them. Tap on your lower abdomen for 10 minutes.

After completing the tapping, place your hands gently on your lower abdomen, moving them in a clockwise direction. Then, keeping your hands there, close your eyes and focus intently on your body's sensations. Notice the rise and fall of your stomach beneath your hands, feeling a warmth spreading across your lower abdomen and back as if something is expanding inside. This will lead to your breath deepening and becoming more relaxed.

Tapping on your lower abdomen energizes and strengthens it, helping you feel more grounded. This practice brings a deep sense of calm and stability. Often we detach from our bodies when we face physical pain, emotional distress, or overwhelming external pressures as our attention gets pulled toward these disturbances. Concentrating on tapping the lower abdomen anchors your energy. This enables you to observe any physical, mental, or emotional discomfort without identifying with it, thus maintaining a clear and observant perspective.

JOURNAL PROMPTS

1. What physical sensations did you notice during and after the exercise?
2. Reflect on any emotions that surfaced during the tapping exercise.
3. How did your level of self-awareness change during the exercise? Did you find yourself becoming more attuned to your body's senses?

Build a Strong Center

Today, you will deepen your practice of establishing a solid energy core in your lower abdomen. Think of this core as a grounding anchor, crucial for holding and stabilizing this area's vital, warm energy, an essential aspect of Water Up, Fire Down energy balance. Without a strong anchor, your energy can become scattered and unfocused, much like a ship that wanders without direction on the open sea. This practice helps you ensure your energy stays centered and grounded, allowing for a more balanced and harmonious flow throughout your body.

When your energy core is unstable, you might find yourself caught in a whirlpool of thoughts and emotions, leading to a disconnection from your body. Essentially, you lose the ability to be fully present, truly inhabit your body, and live in the moment. This is especially true when we're dissatisfied with our current physical, mental, and life circumstances.

The discomfort drives us to escape from ourselves and the present because facing reality can be overwhelming and filled with anxiety, fear, and pain. Consequently, many of us dwell in memories of the past or fantasies about the future, distancing ourselves from the present. This can diminish our capacity to address real-world challenges effectively. It leads to a cycle where things seem to get more complex.

To escape this vicious cycle, bringing yourself back to the present moment is crucial. This week, you've been honing your ability to live in the moment by tuning into your body and sharpening your senses. Today marks the end of your first week dedicated to awakening physical power, and you'll leverage the exercises you've explored to enhance your ability to remain grounded in the now. Let's focus on building the strength to keep your mind in your body, unshaken by fleeting thoughts, emotions, pains, or discomforts.

Exercise: Abdominal Pull & Push

Engage in the Whole Body Shaking exercise for about three minutes while standing. Keep bouncing your knees gently while exhaling through your mouth.

Next, proceed with the Whole Body Tapping. As you maintain the bouncing motion with your knees, tap your arms, chest, stomach, and legs sequentially for about three minutes.

Afterward, transition to Abdominal Tapping using gently clenched fists, alternating between hands. Ensure your shoulders and arms are relaxed as you bounce your knees. Tap your lower abdomen for five minutes, then softly press your palms against your lower abdomen, making circular motions to massage the area.

Move on to today's focus, Abdominal Pull & Push, also known as Intestine Exercise. Position yourself with your feet shoulder-width apart and your knees softly bent.

Place both hands on your lower abdomen, aligning your thumbs with your belly button and bringing your index fingers together to touch lightly. Ensure your shoulders, arms, and hands are relaxed. Tuck your chin, gently close your eyes, and focus on your lower abdomen.

Pull your lower abdomen toward your spine, hold briefly, then gently release, allowing your abdomen to move forward slightly like a balloon. Keep repeating this motion—pulling the lower abdomen back and then pushing it forward, independently of your breathing pattern. Allow your breath to flow naturally as you engage in this deep, rhythmic pull and push. Aim for a deep contraction when pulling in as though your stomach could touch your back. When releasing, do so gently.

As you continue the exercise, be aware of warmth spreading from your lower abdomen and back, dispersing throughout your entire body.

WATCH A VIDEO

After about 10 minutes, gradually cease the abdominal movements while breathing deeply and slowly. Upon completion, gently massage your lower abdomen by making circular motions with your palms.

Place your hands gently on your lower abdomen, focusing inward on your breath. Concentrate on the warm sensation on the surface of your abdomen under your hands and deeper inside. Allow the gentle warmth to spread throughout your abdomen, slowly reaching your entire body with each deep breath. Continue this breathing exercise for 1–2 minutes.

Abdominal Pull & Push will guide you to a state of calm and being grounded. After the exercise, you'll observe your mouth becoming moist, your mind becoming clearer, and a feeling of relaxation in your chest.

Conclude the exercise by taking a few deep breaths.

JOURNAL PROMPTS

1. Did you notice any changes in your physical condition after completing the exercise?
2. What sensations did you feel in your lower abdomen during the exercise?
3. Did you experience any emotional shifts during or after the exercise?

CHAPTER 10

WEEK 2 OPENING YOUR HEART

Last week was all about reconnecting with your body, your sacred temple. You practiced being present by awakening your bodily senses and focusing your awareness on them. You noticed any discomfort and pain, recognizing their presence without identifying with them.

Through the practice of tapping, you've learned to remain grounded in your body, building the resilience to rise above pain and fear, and moving closer to your true self. Along the way, you've activated your body's energy and restored Water Up, Fire Down energy balance. I hope the exercises and meditations you've engaged in have helped you deepen your connection with your body and yourself.

If last week's healing journey didn't unfold as you had hoped, there's no need to worry. The key is perseverance—by not giving up, you're guaranteed to make progress on your healing path. Trust in the journey, tap into your deep-seated desire for genuine healing and transformation, and continue to move forward.

Dealing with emotions can often feel like navigating a stormy sea. Sometimes, it feels like the emotions are throwing our ship off course rather than being a positive force we can harness. The first step toward regaining control of the ship is to acknowledge and feel your emotions since they indicate areas within you that need care and healing. Embracing these feelings helps you connect with yourself on a deeper level.

This week, we'll apply the same focused approach we used to enhance our physical power to understand our emotional landscape. It's common to suppress emotions, especially those linked to painful experiences, but these emotions don't simply disappear. Instead, they can become stored in our bodies, sometimes manifesting as physical discomfort.

Our focus for the second week will be to reflect upon memories of difficult experiences, feeling the emotions and any associated physical discomfort. The goal is to allow ourselves to experience both the emotions and physical discomfort fully. During the process, we'll leverage our ability to sense energy. This approach allows us to take a step back from the raw intensity of our emotions, offering a perspective of calmness and clarity.

Accepting and releasing these emotions and pains lead to a profound sense of freedom, self-love, and confidence. This process uncovers the limitless love within our hearts, laying the foundation for true emotional well-being and a deeper connection with ourselves.

8 Feel Your Heart

Today, you'll dedicate time to connecting with the energy of your heart while also taking a closer look at your emotional landscape. Every emotion carries its unique energy, and leaving them behind is difficult. Powerful emotions, like anger, resentment, anxiety, sadness, self-doubt, and shame, often come from soul-crushing experiences or events. These emotions can substantially impact the energy center of your heart. However, if you fail to express these emotions and choose to repress them instead, they start to weigh heavily on your heart's energy.

First, you'll begin by activating and grounding your body through the Whole Body Tapping you learned last week. Then, you'll move into a guided meditation designed to tune you into the energy of your heart. From this week onward, I encourage you to tap in a way that feels right when you do Whole Body Tapping rather than sticking to the precise sequence we used before. Trust your body's inherent wisdom—it knows what you need for healing and growth. Today, let's take the opportunity to listen to that wisdom by homing in on the heart's energy.

Meditation: Heart Awakening

Tap your whole body with open palms or fists in a standing posture. Let your senses guide where and how you tap, moving around to spots that need attention—whether they're aching, tired, or just enjoyable to touch.

Exhale deeply with each tap, imagining all the stagnant energy leaving your body. Aim to tap all over to ensure energy flows freely everywhere. If some areas feel very tight or sore, spend more time there to aid in relief. Thoroughly tap all parts of your body for about 10 minutes.

After finishing the tapping, sit comfortably in a chair or on the floor with your back straight. Place one hand over the other and rest them in the center of your chest. Relax your shoulders and arms. Notice the warmth of your hands and the gentle rise and fall of your chest as you breathe. Visualize your breath moving into and out of your heart space, fostering openness and warmth.

Continue breathing deeply, gently guiding your focus inward to the center of your heart. As you do, imagine your heart slowly opening and softening with the ease of every breath. Each inhale brings more light and openness into your heart. With every exhale, envision the barriers around your heart dissolving, allowing its energy to flow more freely.

Quietly ask your heart a few questions, leaving room for any responses or sensations that may arise: How have I been feeling emotionally lately? What emotions am I clinging to that no longer serve me? Are there any grudges or resentments I need to release?

Spend a few minutes in silence, open to any insights your heart may provide. Trust that whatever comes up is essential for your awareness and healing. As you focus on your breaths, acknowledge any emotions that may arise, observing them without judgment, simply recognizing them for what they are. When you feel strong emotions like anger, sadness, or fear, imagine them being held gently by the light in your heart. Allow yourself to express these emotions in this safe and nurturing space.

Visualize a warm, glowing light emanating from your hands into your heart. With each breath, this light grows brighter, filling your heart with love and gratitude. Take a moment to thank yourself for dedicating time to connect with your heart space.

When you feel ready, slowly lift your hands from your chest and place them on your knees. Take a few deep breaths to conclude the meditation.

JOURNAL PROMPTS

1. What emotions have you felt the most lately?
2. Are there any feelings you're holding on to that aren't helping you anymore?
3. Do you have any grudges or complicated feelings that are hard to release?

Yesterday, you focused your attention on feeling the energy of your heart space and understanding its contents. Today, you'll dedicate time to releasing the heavy and frustrating energy accumulated within your heart through tapping.

Our heart space is boundless, infinitely scalable, and capable of embracing anything. Yet, if unresolved emotional energies from the past linger and stagnate within it, our heart space becomes cluttered, constricted, and eventually closed off.

When our hearts close, we find ourselves replaying unhelpful or even destructive self-talk repeatedly. We use various defenses to shield ourselves, viewing the world as a harsh battlefield. Consequently, we struggle to welcome new experiences and grow distant from true joy and a sense of aliveness.

Today, take a moment to tap your chest and release any pent-up emotions stored there. While tapping, memories of stressful times may resurface, evoking emotions like anger, sadness, and resentment. Embrace whatever arises. With each exhale, release the energy from your chest, allowing it to leave your body. This process will enable your heart space to expand further. Remember, you can only fill it by emptying it first, and you can only welcome the new by letting go of the old.

Exercise: Chest Tapping

In a standing posture, engage in Whole Body Tapping for 10 minutes. Tap freely, focusing on areas that feel tense or uncomfortable without adhering to a specific order. If you encounter a painful or uncomfortable area, tap that area more. While tapping, gently bounce your knees up and down as you breathe out through your mouth.

After the tapping, sit comfortably with a straightened back, either in a chair or on the floor.

With your right hand in a fist, gently tap the left side of your chest. Close your eyes and continue tapping beneath your left collarbone and along your left rib cage, focusing on the chest's energy. As you tap, open your mouth to release an "Ahh" sound, allowing the vibrations to deepen your experience further.

Switch hands and tap the right side of your chest with your left fist, making an "Ahh" sound.

Clasp your hands and tap the center of your chest with the knuckle of your thumbs, ensuring your shoulders are relaxed. Focus on making the sound of "Ahh" as deeply as possible while exhaling through your mouth.

WATCH A VIDEO

If any emotions or memories arise, allow them to surface and observe them as they are without analyzing or suppressing them. With each exhale, release the energy from your chest.

Tap all over your chest freely with your palms, using either hand that feels comfortable. Focus on exhaling deeply, imagining stress and heavy energy leaving your body with each tap. Keep tapping for about 10 minutes to benefit from the practice fully.

After tapping, place both hands on your chest and focus on breathing for 1–2 minutes. Feel your chest rise and fall with each breath, sensing the warmth from your palms entering your heart. Notice how your chest relaxes and your breathing deepens.

Take a few more deep breaths before finishing.

JOURNAL PROMPTS

1. Did you notice any changes in your chest while tapping and afterward?
2. What emotions and thoughts surfaced during the practice?
3. Did the tapping help you notice any repeated stress or emotional patterns in your life?

DAY 10 Tune into Your Energy Senses

Today, you'll discover the art of sensing energy, a powerful skill in unlocking emotional release and fostering self-love. Sensing energy helps you explore your inner world and understand yourself better. The feeling of expansion, openness, and freedom that comes with it reflects your true nature, showing you who you are at your core.

As you tune into your energy, you free yourself from being overwhelmed by your emotions. This awareness allows you to step back and observe your feelings from a more objective standpoint. It's like finding a calm center amid the chaos of emotions. Feeling energy allows you to maintain a grounded and stable presence.

By detaching from your emotions, you manage them instead of being overwhelmed. Rather than letting your feelings dictate your actions, you can recognize them and respond appropriately. This doesn't mean you should try to control your emotions, but rather that you can learn to understand and accept them, expressing them healthily. This process empowers you to lead an emotionally healthy life, freeing you from the burdens of emotions that once weighed you down.

Meditation: Hand Energy Awakening

Sit comfortably in a chair or on the floor with your back straight. Use your palms to tap your entire body for five minutes. No specific order is required; just ensure you cover all areas evenly.

Following the Whole Body Tapping, spend five minutes tapping on your chest. Remember to keep exhaling and making the "Ahh" sound. Once you've finished tapping your chest, place your hands on your knees and take a few deep breaths.

Bring your palms to chest level, relax your wrists, fingers, and shoulders, and tap your fingertips together for one minute.

Then, with both hands upright, rotate your wrists, twisting them repeatedly for one minute. Breathe out any tension.

Bring your hands 2–3 inches above your knees with your palms up, ensuring your arms are free and not touching the sides of your body. Bring your focus to your palms and very slightly move your hands up

WATCH A VIDEO

and down. You might begin to notice sensations such as tingling, warmth, pressure, prickling, pulsing, or a feeling similar to touching cotton candy in your hands.

Now, very slowly turn your hands so your palms face each other, about two inches apart. Hold them there and continue feeling warmth, tingling, and pulsing between your palms.

Slowly pull the palms of your hands apart and bring them back together, without letting them touch. Continue this motion, ensuring your hands move together and apart slowly.

Extend this feeling to your arms as you become more attuned to energy. You may experience sensations like wearing long gloves around your hands and arms or moving your hands through warm water. Repeat opening and closing the distance between your hands to feel the energy for about 3–5 minutes.

Bring your palms close to your chest, leaving a slight space between your palms and your chest. Feel the energy between your palms and your heart, sensing the warmth as it permeates your chest. Take comfortable breaths for 1–2 minutes, allowing your chest to open and expand.

Afterward, place both hands comfortably on your lap, noticing any sense of peace and tranquility that arises. Take a few deep breaths before concluding the practice.

JOURNAL PROMPTS

1. Describe the sensations you felt during the meditation.
2. How did you feel different mentally after the training?
3. Could you observe your thoughts or emotions without getting caught up in them?

Today, you'll engage in a meditation to connect with a specific emotion that you frequently experience. This emotion may have surfaced recently or lingered for a long time, resurfacing repeatedly. The narrative and context surrounding this emotion are likely familiar, possibly accompanying you for years or even decades.

I call these repetitive patterns that hold us back "emotional past prints." These emotions can hinder our growth and ability to change, often leading us to doubt our worth or capabilities.

Today's meditation lets you understand your emotional patterns and how they've impacted your life. And more importantly, it allows you to release these patterns consciously. As you let go of the weight of past emotional burdens, you unveil the beauty and resilience that lie beneath and open yourself to new opportunities and growth.

This process helps you become the best version of yourself. Freed from the past, you fully engage in the present, crafting your own narrative and realizing your deepest dreams.

Meditation: Four Healing Phrases

Sit comfortably with your back straight, whether in a chair or on the floor. Tap your entire body gently for three minutes using the palms of your hands. There's no need to follow a specific order; tap evenly across your body.

After tapping your entire body, focus on your chest. Use your palms or fists to tap the center of your chest for three minutes. Ensure you evenly tap on the left and right sides of your chest. As you tap, continue to exhale and make the "Ahh" sound.

Now, practice the Hand Energy Awakening you learned yesterday for five minutes. Begin by facing your palms toward each other in front of your chest. Feel the energy as you move your hands further apart and closer together, expanding the feeling between your palms. Focus on this sensation, allowing the energy to grow from your hands to your arms, opening your heart space.

After practicing feeling the energy, place your hands comfortably on your knees with palms up. Close your eyes, straighten your spine, and relax as you focus on breathing.

Take a moment to bring up memories of past challenges or instances where you felt hurt by others or faced difficult situations. Rather than straining to think, allow the first memory that comes to mind to surface naturally.

Vividly recall the person or people involved in the situation that caused you pain. Remember the details of the problem, including what was being said or done and the emotions you experienced. Allow yourself to fully immerse in these memories, acknowledging their impact on you.

As you revisit these memories, pay attention to the emotions that surface within you. Allow yourself to fully acknowledge and experience these emotions without trying to push them away or avoid them.

As you explore these emotions, notice any physical sensations like tightness, pain, or discomfort in your body. Place your hands on or near these areas to focus on them. If you can't reach a specific spot, choose a nearby location representing the discomfort.

Start communicating with the part of your body that harbors the pain or discomfort. You can do this silently or aloud, depending on what feels suitable for you.

Begin by acknowledging the presence of discomfort or pain. Say to yourself or the affected part of your body, "I feel you." Recognize that you may have been neglecting or pushing aside these sensations and emotions; this acknowledgment is the first step toward addressing them.

Tell yourself that it's okay to experience this pain and these emotions. Remind yourself that feeling the way you do is natural and valid. This step is about granting your body and heart permission to express what has been suppressed or held back.

Now, you will use four healing phrases to connect with your body. These phrases originate from Ho'oponopono, a Hawaiian practice of reconciliation and forgiveness. This method is incredibly powerful, especially when combined with energy work.

Start by expressing "I'm sorry," to your body. For instance, "I'm sorry for allowing you to endure this pain." "I apologize for neglecting your needs." "I regret not listening to you." "I apologize for harboring resentment toward you."

Continue by asking for forgiveness. Say, "Please forgive me for abandoning you." "Forgive me for holding on to this pain." "I ask for your forgiveness for running away from your suffering." Listen to your true essence within your body, your soul, as it speaks to you. It may say, "I forgive you," or "It's okay."

Now, express gratitude to your body and yourself. Say, "Thank you," and genuinely appreciate your body for being with you, supporting you, and not giving up on you. Thank your body for allowing you to breathe and exist, even during pain. Acknowledge your body's resilience and unwavering presence, despite any neglect it may have experienced. Feel the warmth of love and healing energy filling your heart as you express this gratitude.

Now, you might want to say: "I love you." Regardless of past neglect or pain, acknowledge the deep care and love you hold for your body and yourself. Feel the sincerity of these phrases as they resonate within you. Allow love to overflow from your heart, enveloping your entire being. Experience this love spreading throughout your body, infusing you with joy, strength, and gratitude. Feel the warmth and healing power of love, embracing your pain, soothing it with compassion and understanding.

Place your hands on your knees, take a few deep breaths, and conclude the meditation.

JOURNAL PROMPTS

1. Which past events arose during the meditation?
2. What emotions did you connect with during today's meditation?
3. Write about your experience and awakening during the Four Healing Phrases meditation.

12 Heal Your Inner Child

Inside each of us is an inner child, the keeper of our early life memories and emotions. This inner aspect fuels your vitality, creativity, and wonder, yet also holds deep fears, unmet needs, and unresolved traumas from childhood. Today's focus is connecting with this part of yourself to release your emotional past prints and deepen the healing process from past trauma.

For those who have experienced intense trauma in childhood, meeting the inner child can be challenging and painful. However, it's crucial to allow yourself to fully experience the difficult emotions stemming from the trauma without judgment or avoidance. Approach this encounter with the utmost kindness and compassion toward yourself.

Fully connecting with your inner child may take time, so be patient with yourself and trust the process. Before beginning this meditation, you will first ground yourself in your body through tapping and feeling energy.

Meditation: Inner Child Embrace

Sit comfortably in a chair or on the floor and start Whole Body Tapping for three minutes. Allow your hands to tap freely, without following any specific order, reaching wherever feels natural.

Next, spend three minutes tapping your chest with fists, followed by another three minutes tapping your solar plexus, located in your upper abdomen just below the ribcage meeting point. Since the solar plexus is sensitive, moderate the strength of your tapping as needed. As you exhale, visualize releasing the heavy, stagnant energy from the tapped areas through your mouth.

Proceed to do Abdominal Tapping using your fists. Alternate your fists to tap your lower abdomen for three minutes rhythmically. Remember to relax your jaw and shoulders as you tap throughout the exercise.

Spend the next five minutes practicing Hand Energy Awakening. Bring your hands close together then apart in front of your chest, sensing the energy between your palms. Feel the energy expanding, your chest opening, and the energy spreading through your arms and body.

After sensing the energy, position your palms facing your chest with a 2–3 inch gap between your hands and chest. Feel the power flowing from your hands into your chest as you prepare for meditation.

Gently close your eyes, straighten your spine, and imagine an energy line extending upward, connecting you to the sky, while grounding yourself through the connection of your sit bones to the earth beneath you. Take deep breaths in and out, allowing each breath to make you feel more relaxed and present.

Reflect on a recurring emotion that challenges you, such as sadness, loneliness, anger, or feelings of abandonment or rejection. Pay attention to where in your body this emotion manifests or impacts you the most.

Recall a moment from your childhood or distant past when you may have initially felt this emotion. Visualize your younger self experiencing the events associated with these feelings as if watching a vivid movie reel of your past.

As you revisit this memory, let the emotions it triggers resurface. Allow these feelings to emerge without resistance or judgment, experiencing their full intensity. The goal of this process is not to dwell on pain but to understand and process your emotions, eventually releasing them.

Take a moment to reflect on what your younger self genuinely needed in that challenging moment. Perhaps it was a hug, someone to listen to, or a comforting presence.

With unwavering compassion, offer your younger self precisely what they need. Feel the weight of your arms wrapping around them in a warm embrace, offering the love and support they longed for. Let them feel your steady and reassuring heartbeat as you provide the comfort they need.

As you hold your younger self in your arms, let your words flow from the depths of your heart, carrying with them the wisdom and compassion of your present self. "Everything will be okay." "You are precious beyond measure, and I care for you deeply." Feel the weight of each word as it resonates with yourself.

With each heartfelt utterance, feel the healing energy coursing through you, bridging the gap between past and present and nurturing your inner child's heart. Embrace them tightly, letting them know they are not alone and deeply loved and cherished.

Gently let go of the visualization of your inner child, resting your hands on your knees. Feel the burdens of the past begin to lighten, replaced by a profound sense of peace and acceptance. With each breath in, affirm, "I love you" to yourself.

Take a few more deep breaths in and out, and when you're ready, open your eyes. Rub your hands together to create warmth, then gently sweep your face, neck, and chest, releasing any remaining tension.

JOURNAL PROMPTS

1. What were the past events and emotions that came up during the meditation?
2. What message did you give your inner child, and how did it feel to give them what they needed?
3. Reflect on any awakenings and insights you gained about yourself during the meditation.

13 Uncover Your Negative Self-Talk

Our internal dialogue, often called "self-talk," is a powerful tool for understanding our feelings and thoughts. This ongoing conversation with ourselves profoundly influences our journey of growth and healing. Within this narrative lies the potential to uplift or hold us back.

Negative stories and thoughts we carry within us can be like heavy chains, holding us back from reaching our full potential. They shape how we see ourselves and the world, affecting every aspect of our lives. These negative narratives act as barriers, making it harder for us to move forward and damaging our self-esteem.

This negative self-talk often originates from our deepest fears, anxieties, and self-critical beliefs. Phrases like, "I'm not good enough," "I'm a failure," or "I can't do anything right," echo in our minds, sabotaging our confidence and preventing us from embracing new challenges or seeking change. Moreover, this persistent negative dialogue amplifies stress and anxiety, impairing our emotional well-being and diminishing our overall quality of life.

To move past the negative stories holding back our growth and healing, we first need to recognize these thoughts for what they are. It's important to realize that these thoughts aren't truths and that our inner voice can sometimes mislead us.

Today, your focus will be on exploring the root of the negative self-talk that often consumes your mind. You'll begin to peel back layers to uncover what's at the core of these unhelpful narratives. Dive deep, and observe what's there.

Meditation: Identifying Inner Negativity

Sit in a chair or on the floor and engage in Whole Body Tapping for three minutes. Tap across your body freely, without following any specific order.

Spend 10 minutes doing Abdominal Tapping, using alternating fists to tap your lower abdomen rhythmically. Focus on exhaling to release heavy, stagnant energy from your body through your mouth.

Move into Hand Energy Awakening for five minutes. Bring your hands together and separate them in front of your chest, sensing the energy between your palms. Feel the energy expand, your chest open, and the energy flow through your arms and body.

After completing Hand Energy Awakening, rest your hands on your knees and breathe comfortably.

Now, take a moment to look inward and consider the voices you hear inside. Your experiences, thoughts, and emotions shape these voices, often going unnoticed. What are the recurring statements you find yourself saying to yourself most frequently? These reflect deeply ingrained beliefs about yourself and your capabilities. Pay close attention to these stories, as they offer valuable insights into your self-perception.

As you tap into the prominent emotion you've been feeling, allow it to guide you toward the thoughts accompanying it. These thoughts may manifest as self-critical statements like, "I'm not good enough," or "I can't trust myself."

Observe your reactions to these thoughts and the emotions they evoke in you. Notice any resistance or discomfort that arises but refrain from judgment. Instead, accept these feelings and thoughts, allowing them to unfold without interference.

Take a few deep breaths to conclude the practice. Warm your hands by rubbing them together, then softly brush over your face, neck, and chest to ease any lingering tension.

JOURNAL PROMPTS

1. What are the specific negative statements you identified during the meditation?

2. Reflect on how often these statements surface in your daily life and in what situations they are most likely to appear.

3. Remember when you first started telling yourself this for each piece of negative self-talk you've identified. Can you identify any events, experiences, or influences that may have contributed to these beliefs about yourself?

This week, you've developed energy senses to feel and expand your heart space. You've dedicated time to healing your inner child by acknowledging childhood events at the root of your emotional challenges. Moreover, you've identified the negative self-talk you often engage in, marking another step toward emotional healing.

Now, let's focus on releasing the emotional pain holding you back, deepening your self-understanding, and embracing compassion, love, and trust. It's the right time to move beyond memories and limiting beliefs.

If you're holding on to resentment toward someone who hurt you, or blaming yourself for past mistakes, consider letting them go.

You don't need their apology or forgiveness to move on. Because you love yourself and your life and you wish to free your soul from the burden of hatred and resentment, you can choose to release any resentment toward that person or yourself. This is possible because you are no longer tied to the past and are eager to move forward. You have the power to break free from the past and look ahead because true freedom for your soul comes from within, not from the actions of the person who has caused you pain.

Choosing to release old emotional energies and limiting self-beliefs that don't support your healing and growth is a courageous act. This choice will bring you closer to your true self and genuine healing.

Meditation: Letting Go

Find a comfortable space where you can sit and move freely. Sit on a chair or in a half-lotus position on the floor with your back straight and close your eyes.

Start by doing Abdominal Tapping with your fists for 10 minutes. Alternate your fists to tap your lower abdomen rhythmically. As you tap, consciously relax your jaw and shoulders, using exhaling breaths to release any stagnant energy.

Next, engage in Hand Energy Awakening for five minutes. Sense the energy between your palms as you move them closer together and then apart. Allow this energy to grow, extending through your arms and into your entire body.

After the energy meditation, sit up straight, place your hands on your knees with palms facing up, and concentrate on deep, slow breaths. Inhale and exhale deeply to guide your mind and body into a more relaxed state.

Begin by identifying the things you're holding on to—ideas or beliefs that bring your energy down. These might be linked to old relationships, negative thoughts about yourself, or ongoing problems at work. Take note if you see these patterns repeating, as it could suggest that you're gripping on to something that needs to be released.

Reflect on recurring stories you tell yourself, whether about feeling inadequate, believing someone hates you, or recalling painful memories. Also, think about any resentment you hold toward individuals who have caused you pain. Bring these thoughts to the forefront and allow yourself to experience any emotions they stir up without suppressing them.

See that holding on to these emotions and narratives impedes your healing progress. Choose to let go now. Say to yourself, "I let you go," freeing yourself from anyone or any situation. Declare, "I am free from you," and for situations, "I release you." Notice the space created by this release. As you continue focusing on your breath, with each exhalation, let go of any tension or lingering emotions in your heart.

Express gratitude for the chance to let go and for the lessons learned. Appreciate the opportunity to change and grow. Say, "Thank you," and feel a sense of expansion and freedom enveloping you.

Take a few more deep breaths before concluding the meditation.

JOURNAL PROMPTS

1. What did you let go?
2. How did you feel immediately after saying, "I let you go"?
3. Do you still have any lingering feelings you haven't released?

CHAPTER 11

WEEK 3 ILLUMINATING YOUR BRAIN

As we enter the final week of our 21-day healing journey, I encourage you to fully immerse yourself in each new exercise and integrate the ones you've previously explored.

To reach your true potential, you must let go of what no longer serves you and has been holding you back. Stay connected with your body and continue practicing sensing and expanding energy to deepen your awareness. Come back home to yourself by bringing awareness to your body and observing the feelings that the energy senses create inside your body.

With this added awareness, you detach from the pain or discomfort of your physical and emotional bodies. You acknowledge them, but you can let them go. This allows you to access the deepest parts of yourself where you can create the life you desire. You will continue to access these beautiful parts of yourself.

In this final week, you'll concentrate on letting your true self guide you forward to connecting you with your inner light or divine energy and the unconditional love they offer. This boundless love and light are already a part of you, waiting to be discovered and embraced.

You'll engage in various exercises designed to awaken your brain. Understand that the brain is more than a physical organ; it is an energetic and spiritual hub where body, mind, and soul converge, a source of creation that transcends physiological functions.

Your brain is a bridge to your life's inherent beauty and completeness, tapping into the wisdom and intelligence you're born with. Your brain is a link to the powerful, natural forces that keep things in balance amid constant change. It opens the door to unlimited creative possibilities and divinity in the universe. By embracing these aspects of your brain, you can unlock the true light within yourself and reach your full potential.

This week, you're focusing on awakening your brain and tapping into universal energy—the divine force that transcends individual existence and unites all life. This energy is both within and around us. You fill your body and mind with love, joy, and creative vibrations by aligning yourself with it.

This week's focus is deeply rooted in spiritual connection. Spirituality begins with the understanding that our reality extends beyond physical form; we are intertwined with infinite energy and consciousness. It's about mastering our lives and shaping them according to our intentions rather than being controlled by limiting patterns of thought, emotion, and behavior. Recognizing that our authentic essence is love, we open ourselves to it and strive to share love with those around us in our daily lives.

When deeply understanding this spirituality, we avoid complaining about physical, emotional, and mental pains. Instead, we learn to navigate through them by accepting and finding ways to grow from them. As we truly practice this, we realize that genuine healing is already occurring within us, regardless of whether our symptoms improve or persist.

15 Walk through Your Life

Today, you will take a moment to reflect on your life journey. From your earliest memories to the present, take time to look back and envision where you're headed.

The Sedona Mago Center has a staircase of 120 steps set along a gentle hill. Inspired by Ilchi Lee's book *I've Decided to Live 120 Years*, these steps symbolize a life of fulfillment lived authentically and purposefully. Each step represents a year of your life, prompting you to reflect on your journey as you ascend. You will visualize walking up these stairs in your mind.

During this meditation, it's crucial to approach your past with calm and objectivity. Reflect on the important moments and events that have shaped your life, including those that brought pride, joy, and regrets.

There may be memories or traumas you'd rather not revisit. Because you've practiced confronting and accepting physical and emotional pain without avoidance, adopting an observant stance, you'll now be able to grasp the meaning of those events from a different perspective. While the painful memory still exists in your personal history, it will feel different to you now.

This realization will resonate deeply in your heart: "The life I've lived so far is uniquely mine. Every moment has contributed to shaping who I am today. This journey belongs to me, and no one else." Reflecting on your life with this mindset, you'll feel genuine gratitude for the time, experiences, and people you've encountered.

Above all, you'll feel profound gratitude and love for yourself, having experienced every moment in life that led you to the present. Even the most painful moments will be embraced with gratitude as you understand their significance. Viewing your life through this lens gives you a fresh perspective on your future, clarifying what you want as you move forward.

Meditation: Steps of Life Reflection

Find a comfortable position seated on a chair or floor. Dedicate the next 10 minutes to Abdominal Tapping, tapping your lower abdomen with your fists, alternating between them. Having engaged in this exercise for several days, you may find it increasingly easier to slip into its rhythm.

Afterward, perform a five-minute Hand Energy Awakening. As the sensation of energy grows, it will extend beyond your arms, encompassing your torso and spreading throughout your entire body. You may feel an urge to move your body in specific ways; follow these sensations and move accordingly.

After feeling the energy, place your hands on your knees with your palms facing up. Sit straight, relax your chest and shoulders, and gently close your eyes. Keep your chin slightly tucked in to align your spine and head. Start by focusing on your body from your head to your lower abdomen. Take your time to scan through each part, breathing naturally as you go.

Imagine yourself in a place surrounded by beautiful red rocks. The sky is intensely blue, the air is crisp, and you smell the scent of sage in the air. Before you, a beautiful staircase of 120 steps ascends a low hill.

Begin by standing at the threshold of the first step. With each breath, draw in the earth's energy, grounding yourself in the present moment. Feel the connection to your surroundings as you prepare for the first step.

As you ascend the first set of steps, reflect on your earliest memories. Recall the moments of being held and loved and the simplicity of childhood joys. Allow these memories to fill you with warmth and a sense of belonging.

If you had difficult times in your early years, acknowledge them fully. Remember that you've already confronted those memories and released associated emotions, allowing you to recall them with less pain now.

Continue forward, reaching the steps marking your teenage years. Contemplate the desires, dreams, and challenges of this time. What mattered most to you then? What actions did you take in pursuit of what you wanted? Acknowledge the journey, achievements, and unmet desires, embracing them with compassion.

As you progress, the steps lead you into your twenties and thirties, significant decades of change, growth, and possibly loss. Reflect on the pivotal moments, awakenings, and search for meaning. What were you seeking sincerely within? Recognize the evolution of your desires and the paths you choose.

Consider the essence of your life's purpose by approaching the steps representing your forties and beyond. What drives you? In this moment, what is it that you wish to manifest? Speak this intention silently to yourself, affirming your commitment to your true self.

Now, visualize yourself ascending the steps beyond your current age, into your sixties, seventies, eighties, and even beyond. With each step, feel fulfilled by living a life true to yourself. See the love and joy you share expanding, touching the lives of those around you, fostering hope within your community and beyond.

Gently rest your hands on your chest and focus on your breath. Let gratitude overflow within your heart. Feel the profound love you hold for yourself and your life. Sense your inner longing to infuse your journey with fulfillment, love, and joy. Conclude the meditation with a few deep breaths.

JOURNAL PROMPTS

1. Which specific event from your life stood out the most during this meditation?
2. Have you experienced any realizations or insights about past events that caused you pain?
3. When envisioning your future, what value is most important to you?

Today, take the time to discover what you truly desire by connecting with your true self. Your true self holds the answers to your deepest desires. It simply knows without seeking external information.

Although our surface desires may vary from person to person, we share common aspirations at our core. We all crave love and connection and long for the freedom to live authentically and express ourselves. This is because, fundamentally, we are beings driven by love, which is inherent. Our deepest fulfillment arises when we fully express and embrace our true selves.

Genuine self-love isn't a task to accomplish. It's not something external to attain; it's an intrinsic part of who you are. True self-love patiently resides beneath the layers of thoughts, emotions, and external influences. Its clarity emerges when you peel away the barriers that obstruct your connection to your authentic self.

Your true self is rooted in love, untouched by pain, trauma, inadequacy, or self-doubt. Today, connect with this enduring love that transcends thoughts and emotions. You're incorporating Brain Wave Vibration, a cornerstone exercise of Brain Education. This dynamic meditation entails gently moving your head from side to side while tapping the lower abdomen as you've been practicing. It's known to be effective in awakening the three energy centers of your body—the lower abdomen, heart, and brain, all at once.

Exercise: Brain Wave Vibration

Sit on a chair or on the floor. Keep your back straight, relax your chest and shoulders, and rest your hands on your knees with your palms facing upward. Close your eyes gently and bring your chin slightly inward.

Start by focusing your attention on your body's sensations from within. Begin at the top of your head, then move downward, mentally scanning through your head, neck, and spine. Progress slowly, scanning your entire body until you reach your lower abdomen.

Direct your attention to your lower abdomen. Lightly clench your fists and start doing Abdominal Tapping with alternating hands. As you tap, allow your head, spine, and upper body to move naturally with the tapping.

After about three minutes, once you've settled into a rhythm, gently shake your head from left to right while tapping your lower abdomen. Initiate the head movement gently and slowly, avoiding any forceful or rapid actions.

WATCH A VIDEO

Shake your head gently to release tension from your neck to your shoulders. Gradually increase the speed of the shaking while tapping your lower abdomen. If you feel heavy or hot energy in your head, exhale through your mouth to release it.

As you continue to breathe out, your breathing becomes lighter and more natural. This helps to open up any blocked energy in your chest and relieve tension.

Continue tapping your lower abdomen and moving your head left and right for about 10 minutes. Once you feel grounded and sense an activation of energy, you're ready to proceed to the next step.

Silently ask yourself, "What do I want?" Listen to the answers that come to you. Initially, many thoughts and responses may arise. Acknowledge their presence and repeat the question, "What do I want?" Let this question deeply penetrate your heart and mind as you continue doing Brain Wave Vibration.

Summon the courage to enter your heart. Ask sincerely, "What am I truly seeking?" Let the question resonate within you, allowing your heart to respond authentically. Delve into your heart. What do you deeply desire? Ask with utmost sincerity and honesty. This is a moment of full-heart connection. Understand that this connection surpasses knowledge and thoughts. You know it instinctively. What are you truly searching for? Listen to the answers and observe your heart's response. The energy created through Brain Wave Vibration helps you access your inner wisdom, transcending your thoughts and emotions.

When you discover the answers you seek, your heart will resonate with its truth. Embracing and acknowledging this truth will bring confidence, joy, and clarity to your heart. As you discover the answer, your heart will open, and you'll feel a steady stream of love and energy enveloping you. Love pours down onto you, and love springs up from within. You may find tears welling up in your eyes. Open your heart fully and allow yourself to receive the love and blessings. Let your body and mind heal with this love and blessings.

Place your hands over your heart. Feel gratitude welling up within you. "Thank you" and "I love you." Express these words to yourself, feeling their profound significance. With each breath, sense your heart expanding with love and brimming with deep gratitude.

As you conclude, gently lower your hands to your lap. With each inhale, allow a gentle smile to grace your lips. Let this smile symbolize the joy and love you've connected with. Take a few deep breaths and finish.

JOURNAL PROMPTS

1. Reflect on what you discovered about what your heart truly seeks.
2. What are the core desires you identified during the meditation?
3. Reflect on the experience of opening your heart and connecting with your true self.

17 Express Your Love

Today, let's broaden your energy awareness and engage in soul dancing, moving freely within the flow of the energy. This practice is known as Energy Dance.

In these dynamic, flowing movements, you allow the energy to freely guide your body. Sometimes, the dance unfolds slowly and peacefully, like a white crane gliding through a blue sky. Other times, it can be intense and forceful, like a thunderstorm raging in a dark sky. Your body may vibrate, stretch, and twist in unexpected ways. Embrace these movements fully. If needed, stand up and let the energy flow through you. Let your emotions flow and be released.

If you still have lingering feelings in your heart that need release, you may notice them resurfacing as you dance. However, you'll now observe and release them instead of getting lost. Allow yourself to feel these emotions but maintain a sense of detachment and acceptance as you let them go. Keep encouraging yourself to delve deeper inside; over time, you'll experience a profound sense of self-love emanating from within.

As you keep practicing Energy Dance, you'll notice the boundary between yourself and your energy gradually fading. Initially, it might seem like you're moving based on your intention, but soon, your body will start leading the movement independently. Eventually, the distinction between your intention and the movement of energy becomes indistinct, and they flow together seamlessly.

While practicing Energy Dance, avoid suppressing any movements; instead, completely surrender to the experience. With continued practice, the boundary between you as an observer and the observed dissolves, leading to a profound sense of unity within yourself. This brings about a deep understanding of peace and freedom. In these moments, your heart may open, and tears may flow from the depths of your soul. Express these heartfelt emotions through your body, tapping into deep soul feelings that resonate through every cell of your being.

Exercise: Energy Dance

Start Whole Body Shaking from a standing position while maintaining awareness of your body. Feel your body gradually loosening as you continue shaking. Mentally scan your body from head to toe, observing how each part feels as you shake. Let your body relax completely, letting each part dangle and jiggle freely. Do this for three minutes.

WATCH A VIDEO

Tap your entire body with the palms of your hands, allowing your body to bounce lightly. Tap without following any specific order, simply tapping wherever feels uncomfortable or tense. Let your body's instincts guide your hands to the areas that need healing. Continue doing Whole Body Tapping for three minutes.

Now, transition into Abdominal Tapping, allowing your body to move freely in response to the tapping. Let your legs, hips, torso, neck, and shoulders move as needed to release stress and tension. Follow your body's natural rhythm. Continue tapping rhythmically on your lower abdomen while releasing heavy energy through your mouth. After about five minutes of tapping, find a comfortable seated position on a chair or in a half lotus posture on the floor.

Proceed with Hand Energy Awakening. If you prefer, you can play beautiful, soulful music that resonates with you, perhaps something you feel like dancing to.

Bring your hands to your chest, allowing your palms to move toward each other and apart again. Repeat this motion, letting your hands move further apart without consciously controlling the movement. Feel the energy building between your palms, allowing them to express your heart's feelings.

Breathe in as your hands expand away from each other and out as they come closer together. Find a natural rhythm of movement. Continue allowing your hands to move freely, letting your arms circle your body as they naturally desire.

Allow your arms to move freely, and gradually extend this movement to include your torso, head, hips, legs, and feet. Let your entire body flow with the energy you feel. Release any expectations or restrictions on how you should move, and instead, trust in your body's innate wisdom. When you intend to move freely and harmoniously with your body, it will naturally adjust and align to ensure the opening of all energy channels. Do this soulful dance for five minutes.

When you're ready, place one hand on your chest and the other on your abdomen, breathing deeply and slowly for 1–2 minutes. Say, "I love myself," and notice how these words make you feel. Express gratitude to yourself. Gently smile as you feel the warmth in your heart, and slowly lower your hands. Take a few deep breaths to conclude.

JOURNAL PROMPTS

1. Did you notice any changes in your energy or bodily sensations?
2. What emotions did you experience during the practice?
3. Is there anything you learned about yourself through this experience?

18 Invite Universal Energy

Each of us holds immense potential, capable of reaching our unique greatness. However, our established patterns, emotions, thoughts, and habits frequently act as barriers, keeping us from fully realizing our true potential.

So far, you've been rediscovering your true self and identifying the old patterns, habits, emotions, and thoughts that have limited you. You've sharpened your ability to sense energy and have used this skill to move beyond these barriers.

Now, you will explore how to connect with universal energy, the purest form of energy permeating the universe, connecting all things as one. This energy is completely impartial, not influenced by any preferences or judgments. It's a divine energy that is accessible to everyone.

We and all life consist of energy. Energy moves according to your intentions and focus. Energy follows where your mind goes. This energy extends beyond your physical body, traveling anywhere and everywhere, and it's always moving.

You can invite universal energy into your body and your life by clearly setting your intentions and focusing on being receptive. The more you let this universal energy circulate through you, the deeper you enhance your connection, fostering a sense of unity among your mind, body, and soul.

Meditation: Universal Energy Connection

Sit comfortably either on the floor in a half-lotus position or on a chair with your back straight. Start by grounding yourself with Abdominal Tapping for 10 minutes. As you tap your lower abdomen, consciously release tension from your entire body, from your head down to your toes. Focus on each exhale, allowing yourself to sink deeper into a state of relaxation.

Tap into the observer within you, sensing and observing everything from a place of inner calm. With each exhale, allow your body to relax, releasing any stagnant energy.

After completing the Abdominal Tapping, transition into the Energy Dance from yesterday. Start by practicing the Hand Energy Awakening, feeling the energy sensation between your hands and extending it throughout your body, from your arms to your legs and entire body. Move your body freely, following its natural rhythm and the desires of your heart. Dedicate five minutes to this practice.

After your Energy Dance session, sit with your hands resting on your knees, palms facing upward. Ensure your back is straight, your chest and shoulders are relaxed, and gently close your eyes. Pull your chin slightly inward to align your spine and head.

Now, focus on the crown of your head. Imagine a radiant stream of light descending from above and entering your brain. Feel the light permeating the center of your brain and spreading throughout every part of it.

Feel your breath deepening with each inhale and exhale. Sense the brightness intensifying within your brain. Direct your attention to the center of your brain and feel the energy flowing inward. Allow it to cascade down your spinal cord and permeate your entire nervous system, reaching every part of your body. Embrace this flow of light as it saturates your being.

Immerse yourself in the loving embrace of the radiant light, allowing it to penetrate every aspect of your being. As you unite with this divine energy, feel it dissolve any remnants of frustration, lack, negative memories, or lingering emotions in your heart. Let this profound unity heal your body and mind, creating peace and tranquility.

This is the universe's healing energy, permeating every cell of your body. Feel the brightness in your brain and throughout your entire being. Take a few more deep breaths to absorb this energy fully, and then conclude the meditation.

JOURNAL PROMPTS

1. How did universal energy feel in your body?
2. After meditation, how do you feel compared to before?
3. What insights or realizations emerged about your current state of being or life situation?

19 Ask Your Infinite Brain

To tap into your brain's potential, start by asking it big questions about life, such as "Who am I?" and "What is my purpose?" This approach turns your brain into a gateway to discover your deepest truths and untapped potential. By asking your brain meaningful questions, you encourage it to dig deep and come back with insights about who you are and what you're meant to be.

Ask your brain, then confirm with your heart. When you inquire sincerely and earnestly, your brain delivers the inspiration and guidance you need. You can then verify the truth of these answers through the feelings in your heart.

We all possess soulful desires. These are deep, intrinsic wishes and yearnings that resonate with our very essence, distinct from surface-level desires driven by societal norms, materialism, or ego. Such desires are connected to our true selves and our purpose in life. They reflect what truly brings us joy and fulfillment on emotional, spiritual, and existential levels.

Today, you'll ask your brain an important question and listen for its answer. This will help you understand your soulful desires more clearly, helping you make choices confidently.

Meditation: Brain Energy Awakening

Sit on a chair or in a half-lotus posture on the floor and practice Brain Wave Vibration for 10 minutes. Shake your head side to side while tapping your lower abdomen with alternating fists. Continuously release heavy, stagnant energy by exhaling deeply.

Transition into the Hand Energy Awakening. Bring your hands to your chest and widen and narrow the gap between them. Feel the energy between your hands intensify and spread to your arms and torso.

Once you activate the energy field between your hands, cup your hands on either side of your head, keeping a slight distance of about 3–4 inches between them and your head. Repeat gently moving your hands away from your head and drawing them closer. Like how you felt the energy between your hands in the Hand Energy Awakening, now you'll sense the energy between your hands and your brain. Pay attention to various energy sensations, like tingling, pricking, expansion, contraction, and magnetic sensations, not just in your hands but also in your scalp and brain.

Bring your hands before your face and direct healing energy toward it. With your hands positioned slightly away from your face, gently move your palms as if you were washing your face with bright energy, ensuring every corner of your face is enveloped in this healing energy.

Now, gently move your hands from your forehead, tracing the midline of your head up to the top as you channel healing energy into your brain. Then, slowly bring your hands down from the top of your head to the center line at the back, maintaining the energy flow. Now, allow your hands to move freely, guiding the energy to every corner of your brain. Visualize wrapping a radiant energy helmet around your head, noticing the subtle energy sensations throughout your head.

Bring your comfortable hand's index, middle, and ring fingers together and tap the third eye point between your eyebrows for one minute, focusing on the center of your brain. As you tap, you may feel pressure or a gentle throbbing sensation on your forehead, indicating the activation of the third eye, the spiritual energy center in the forehead.

Place your hands on your knees with palms facing up and prepare to receive universal energy. Imagine a radiant stream of light entering through the crown of your head and illuminating the inside of your brain, extending even to your forehead. Focus on allowing this light to penetrate your brain, observing as it brightens your eyes. Feel the incredible light and vibration as it flows through your brain, spine, and entire body.

Experience the clarity, peace, and calmness as the divine light and the power of the universe envelop your brain, body, and the space around you.

Place one hand on your heart and the other on your abdomen. Ask your brain, "Who am I?" Allow your divine essence to respond without hesitation or doubt. Speak to yourself, affirming, "I am ..." and observe what naturally emerges.

In a grounded and centered manner, quietly or aloud, continuously repeat the answer your brain provided. Feel the weight and truth of these words as they resonate deeply within you. Persist until the essence of the phrase permeates every part of your being, anchoring it firmly in your heart. When you're ready, bring your hands to your knees with palms facing up.

Take a few deep breaths to conclude the practice.

JOURNAL PROMPTS

1. What words or feelings came to you when you asked, "Who am I?" during the meditation?
2. How did the affirmation "I am . . ." affect you as you repeated it?
3. How might you integrate the sense of identity you discovered during meditation into your everyday life?

20 Live as Your True Self

Today, you will practice meditation to envision yourself as the person you truly wish to be. This meditation will allow you to hold that vision in your mind's eye, experiencing sensations and energy movements as if you're already living your desired life.

First, you will engage in the experience of connecting with your brain's creative space, stimulating it to function as your vision screen. Then, you will immerse yourself completely in the sensation of living as the best version of yourself, using your five senses to navigate and fully embody this envisioned reality.

During the meditation, feel free to ask your brain any questions. Your brain, aligned with the energy of your highest self, can offer guidance, clarity, and insights to help you navigate the path toward living as your true self. Whether you're looking for advice on overcoming obstacles, seeking clarity about your purpose, or making important life decisions, trust that the answers will come, wrapped in the calm assurance of your inner wisdom.

Meditation: Life Visioning

Sit comfortably in a half lotus posture on the floor or in a chair, and practice Brain Wave Vibration for 10 minutes. Make fists and tap your lower abdomen with alternating hands, while gently shaking your head side to side. Remember to exhale through your mouth to release any heavy, hot energy from your brain.

Next, transition to the Hand Energy Awakening. Begin by bringing your hands in front of your chest and moving them closer and further apart to sense the energy between them. Once you feel the energy intensifying, slowly bring your hands to your forehead.

Allow your palms to face each other without touching, maintaining a distance of about 3–4 inches between them. Practice expanding and contracting your hands, mimicking the movements from the Hand Energy Awakening.

Inhale as you expand your hands in front of your forehead and exhale as you contract them. Coordinate your hand movements with your breathing. Continue this movement, focusing on the strengthening energy of the third eye on your forehead.

As you stimulate your third eye by expanding and contracting the energy, imagine a screen opening in your mind's eye. See it as a movie screen where you are solely the observer.

As you expand and contract your hands, visualize who you genuinely wish to be. Allow this vision to emanate from your highest consciousness. Picture your heart's true desire unfolding. Imagine the version of yourself you've connected with during this week's meditations as if it's already happening in the present moment. Use your five senses to immerse yourself in this vision fully.

Focus on your breath in unison with your hand movements. Envision people, landscapes, places, and times to make this visualization realistic. Allow yourself to feel, think, see, touch, and hear as if it is all happening now.

Now, place your hands close to your chest with your palms facing it. Move your hands gently closer to and away from your chest without touching it. Keep repeating this movement. As you do this, imagine sending love to yourself and picture living your best life, true to who you are.

Send energy and love to the people involved in your visualization, to whomever you consider part of your life. See them happily interacting with you, enjoying your company and collaboration. Feel the confidence in your heart that you will manifest this reality and live as this new version of yourself.

Slowly bring your hands to rest on your chest and express gratitude for this envisioned creation. Feel the growing confidence in your heart as you acknowledge the life you have already begun to create. Clarify in your mind and heart the direction you are headed.

Place your hands on your knees and take a few deep, relaxed breaths to conclude the meditation.

JOURNAL PROMPTS

1. Who did you visualize yourself being in the meditation?
2. Who did you send energy and love to during your meditation?
3. What are you most grateful for from this practice?

Today marks the culmination of our 21-day journey together. In your final session, you'll focus on extending the love and boundless energy you've nurtured within yourself to those around you. You've discovered that love's trustworthy source lies not outside but continuously springs from within you. Love multiplies as you give and share it—such is the nature of love. Waiting passively for love often leads to feelings of sadness, anxiety, and bitterness, especially when the love you seek doesn't arrive. However, when you actively choose to give love, there's no room for such worries; you become the originator of love.

Love comes to life in simple, everyday actions. It's in the warmth of your gaze, your smile's brightness, and your voice's kindness. You share love by offering encouragement, speaking words that build trust, and performing acts of kindness that show you genuinely care.

You can share love through the energy you emit, which is inherently honest. Even if you conceal feelings of dislike and verbally express love for someone, your energy will reveal the truth. It's incapable of deceit. This energy, unbounded by limits, can reach anyone, anywhere, transcending the barriers of time and space.

You can transmit the love, peace, stability, and freedom you experience directly to others through energy. You've heard many incredible stories about how energy has facilitated healing. When you send healing energy with a sincere heart, it can reach and aid in someone's healing. This works because you and the recipient are both naturally attuned to energy and can respond to its influence.

Energy sharing goes beyond just reaching out to people; you can also send it to plants, animals, specific communities, places, or the entire planet and universe. The fascinating part is that when you send out healing energy filled with love, whether to a person, a plant, or any place, you are the first to experience its benefits. This happens because, in sending out this positive energy, you must tap into it, allowing it to fill and uplift you before it moves on to its intended recipient.

Meditation: Golden Light Healing

Find a comfortable space to sit and move your body freely without restrictions. Sit comfortably on a chair or the floor, allowing you to maintain your balance and posture without strain. Close your eyes.

Make fists with both hands and do Abdominal Tapping with alternating hands for 10 minutes. This exercise will help keep you centered and connected to your body.

Spend five minutes tuning into your energy through Hand Energy Awakening before transitioning into the following meditation.

Slowly place your hands near your chest, with your palms facing but not touching your heart. Sense the warm, loving energy radiating from your heart—a love that longs to be extended to others.

With each breath, visualize a bright, golden light of love emanating from your heart. This light surrounds you, forming a beautiful capsule with warmth and light. You find yourself bathed in this divine light, which makes you feel whole and complete.

Expand this golden capsule as you breathe, inviting your loved ones to share in this sacred space filled with light, love, vitality, and hope. Together, bask in the warmth and light, feeling connected and renewed with every shared moment.

As you breathe deeply, the energy capsule grows, extending even further. Openly invite those you've felt distant from, enveloping them in love and energy. Observe as they are uplifted by this shared connection, radiating joy and happiness.

Widen this circle of warmth to include everyone, reaching out to people worldwide. Imagine this golden light wrapping around the Earth, spreading joy and peace to every corner, touching all lives.

As the capsule expands, its edges dissolve, leaving you in an endless expanse of golden light. This boundless energy stretches out, enfolding all creation in waves of love and peace.

Now, extend your arms with palms facing outward, channeling warm, healing energy from your heart. Visualize this as a golden light radiating outward, reaching your loved ones, your community, and beyond to people around the globe. See it expanding to embrace all life on Earth, spreading comfort and peace. Feel a deep connection with all beings as you share this unconditional gift of love and healing.

Bring your hands together in front of your chest, palms touching. With each deep breath, connect with the love in your heart, a love that seeks to reach and embrace every person and creature on this planet.

While breathing in the golden light, hold this prayer or intention in your heart: "May we all come home to our true selves." "May we all feel loved." "May all beings find health, happiness, and peace."

Feel your heart open wide, enveloped in love and light, creating a bond with all life around you. Express gratitude for this moment and the ability to connect deeply with yourself. Recognize your true nature, the sincere longing to love others, and all life on our planet.

Conclude the meditation with a few deep breaths.

JOURNAL PROMPTS

1. Reflect on the feelings and sensations experienced when you create the energy capsule.
2. How did it feel to send love and positive energy to others actively?
3. Reflect on your awakening and transformation after completing the 21-day journey. Write insights, changes, and new understandings you've discovered about yourself and your healing journey.

CHAPTER 12

HEALING CONTINUES

Congratulations on completing your 21-day healing journey. You've done an incredible job, and I'm so happy for you. Each day has brought new exercises, fresh insights, and valuable opportunities for being close to yourself. From harnessing your physical body's power to delving into the depths of your emotions, you've navigated through pain with compassion, recognizing that love is the ultimate healer.

I hope you've experienced clarity, revelation, and a deeper connection with yourself. Even if things didn't unfold exactly as planned, every effort you've put in has been a step forward in your healing journey. This journey has been meaningful if you've gained more insights about who you are.

Regardless of whether you've achieved all your specific goals, your journey speaks volumes about your belief in yourself and your capacity to realize your potential. Rather than just a distant memory, let this experience serve as a solid foundation for continued growth and self-development.

Guidelines for the Next Step

As you stand on the threshold of a new chapter, remember that your journey doesn't have to end here. Exploring the energy principles and practices you've engaged with requires more than one round. Feel free to repeat the 21-day practice as many times as you feel called to do so.

Consistent practice is crucial for staying connected to our true selves and maintaining our energy balance, especially in today's hectic world. Each day presents us with challenges such as work responsibilities, family obligations, and social media interactions, all of which can disrupt our energy flow and pull us away from our authentic selves.

Regardless of how busy life may seem, I encourage you to carve out at least 30 minutes a day for yourself and commit to regular practice. Finding harmony and balance within yourself is critical to maintaining good health. You already have the tools necessary to achieve this balance; now, it's a matter of using them effectively. You can remain calm and centered even amid life's chaos by cultivating self-awareness about your energetic state and taking proactive steps to restore balance when needed.

During the 21-day journey, you started to let go of pent-up emotions, clearing out long-neglected stagnant energy from your heart space. But just like tidying a room once only keeps it clean for a while, regularly tending to our emotional well-being is an ongoing practice. Life keeps throwing challenges our way, stirring up emotions that need addressing. So, make it a habit to carve out time regularly to process and release what's weighing on you. You'll better manage your emotions and stay true to yourself with practice.

Consider Alicia's story as an example. Following the Love Heals Retreat, she remained committed to her practice, and her dedication made a difference. Her migraines, which used to hit her 10–15 times a month, were a constant drain on her, even with medication. But by dedicating herself to the energy practice, she cut the frequency of her migraines in half and lessened their intensity, needing less medication overall. She also successfully reduced her intake of depression medication by half.

Then there's Anna. She lived for years under the shadow of a heart condition, always preparing for the worst. But by weaving the healing tools she learned into her daily routine, she's rewritten her story. "I know I've got the power to keep my heart healthy," she says. "Tomorrow might be uncertain, but I'm choosing to see the beauty in it. And you know what? My body's responding to that positivity." She knows that she has the power to live a full and healthy life.

As you integrate the lessons from your 21-day journey into your daily routine, here are some practical tips to support you on this path:

1. Now that you've journeyed through the healing process and experienced the whole flow, it's time to adopt a more flexible approach. You don't have

to adhere strictly to the order laid out in this book. Take ownership of your healing process by selecting practices that resonate most with you.

2. If you want to enhance the physical aspect of your healing journey, consider incorporating Abdominal Tapping and Abdominal Pull & Push into your daily exercise routine. Dedicate 10 minutes daily to each exercise. It's best to perform these exercises at least an hour after meals to prevent discomfort.

3. I want to emphasize the importance of the foundational practices you've repeated throughout the journey, including Whole Body Shaking, various body tapping exercises, and Brain Wave Vibration. These exercises ground you in your body, preparing you for deeper exploration. The key is to continue these practices until your energy activates and circulates. Spend 10 to 20 minutes on these exercises before moving into meditation.

4. Following these exercises, feel the energy and expand your sensations. The Hand Energy Awakening meditation you've learned helps release emotions and serves as a gateway to your inner truth. From there, dive into meditation to tap into the wisdom of your heart. Your body and heart hold the keys to your true self. Approach them with sincerity and openness, and you'll uncover the answers you seek, paving the way for true healing. Always begin by sensitizing and connecting with your body, the gateway to your heart and soul.

5. While you may have explored these questions during the 21-day journey, continue focusing on who you want to become and where you want to go. Ask yourself, "Who am I?" and "What do I truly desire?" with utmost honesty and sincerity. Challenge yourself to delve deeper into these questions earnestly. They possess the power to strip away the layers of your identity, moving beyond aspects such as your job, personality, ethnicity, and gender. Embrace the answers you discover with conviction and live by them. Although embodying this newfound self-awareness may not happen overnight, you're getting closer to becoming the person you aspire to be.

Live the Love and Light

Healing isn't a destination; it's an ever-unfolding journey. Even as you resolve long-standing issues or overcome past traumas, I hope you understand that this journey isn't about reaching a final destination of perfection. It's about embracing the ongoing process of self-discovery and growth.

As you journey forward, always remember to come home to yourself. In moments of doubt or uncertainty, return to your body and the sanctuary of your heart, where the flame of your true essence burns brightly.

Love yourself and say yes to life unconditionally. Say yes to the adventures that await you, yes to the challenges that will test you, and yes to the limitless possibilities that lie ahead. Through this unwavering affirmation, our energy and consciousness rise, and the essence of our being finds its fullest expression.

When you stand tall, rooted in the soil of your true self, when you show up with authenticity, nothing in the world can strip you of your inherent worth. You can make new choices and create the new life you've been looking for. Trust in yourself, your journey, and the transformative power of love, knowing that the bright light of your true self guides your path.

Living your truth and sharing love inspire others to do the same. Your love spreads, touching hearts and expanding healing around you. As we continue our journey, we realize our role as conduits for the love surrounding us. We learn to open ourselves to love, allow it to fill our hearts, and extend it outward, enriching our world.

With each step you take, may you walk in alignment with your most authentic self, knowing that you carry the love and light that make our world more beautiful. May you always remember that through love, healing becomes possible.

AN INVITATION
TO SEDONA

In some retreats I lead, I guide participants to a special location for sunrise meditation. It's called Mission Place within the Sedona Mago Center. As we journey there, the surroundings are enveloped in pitch-black darkness. We immerse ourselves in the sacred energy that fills Sedona's sky, land, and mountains while awaiting the dawn.

At this moment, an extraordinary stillness surrounds us, deep enough to make even the faintest whisper of our breath audible. As the first rays of light emerge over the mountain's silhouette, an awakening unfolds around us and within us. The morning light doesn't just illuminate the landscape; it ignites a radiant glow within the depths of our being.

As the sun ascends, a bright light floods our senses from within, as if the inner light radiates outward and merges seamlessly with the sunrise. Suddenly, the air fills with the melodious chirping of birds, signaling the arrival of a new day and welcoming us into its embrace.

The juniper trees, cacti, hills, and red rocks seem to rejoice, inviting us to share their celebration of the day's beauty. As if by metamorphosis, we transform from individual observers into an integral part of the unfolding light, internally and externally.

For those fortunate enough to have witnessed this magical moment, it reminds them of the interconnectedness of all life. Each breath of mountain air, every rustle of leaves, fosters a sense of unity that transcends individual existence.

Standing together, witnessing the dawn, and feeling deeply connected to the world, we reflect on our journeys of healing and transformation. Sharing this sunrise is not just a ritual; it symbolizes the personal awakenings experienced in our lives.

Every time I lead the sunrise meditation, I'm deeply moved by how this natural ritual mirrors our process of healing and transformation. Regardless of how dark the previous night might have been, the sun will rise without fail. Witnessing the break of a new day, as the darkness gives way to light, is a powerful reminder that hope is eternal, and every day offers a new beginning.

Welcoming You to Sedona Mago

Hosting the Love Heals Retreat at Mago is a profoundly meaningful experience for me, one that I cannot envision taking place anywhere else. About 20 years ago, during one of the most challenging times of my life, I found solace within its embrace. I was navigating the heartache of infertility, facing one barrier after another. After many medical tests, doctors found that the issue was within me, but they couldn't figure out why I wasn't getting pregnant. Eventually, I opted for a donor egg and became pregnant, only to have a miscarriage just two weeks later. This experience shook me to my core, leaving me feeling shattered, questioning my worth, and grappling with feelings of failure.

Amid my struggles and loss, I had the opportunity to attend a healing retreat at Mago. During one session, I was immersed in the Energy Dance for quite some time. As I engaged in this practice, something remarkable happened. All at once, all my worries, fears, heartache, and pain vanished.

At that moment, there was just me and pure energy. I wasn't just interacting with energy; I was energy itself. Though I couldn't intellectually comprehend the experience, I felt it with startling clarity. The energy surrounded and filled me, growing more intense until I thought there was only energy. Overwhelmed by this sensation, tears welled up uncontrollably, leading to the most intense cry I've experienced in my adult life.

I'll never forget that moment of connection and expansion. It awakened me to my spiritual essence, and I realized I was never broken; I felt so solid and limitless. No one needed to explain it to me—I just understood at that moment. At Mago, I found my true self.

Sedona Mago was where I could set aside everything—the everyday busyness, the social pressures, the roles

I played—and show up as I was. Here, I could shed the protective armor I had built over the years. Every day was a journey toward simplicity, and Mago's beautiful nature embraced me and encouraged me, telling me it was okay just to be myself. It was a place where I could breathe deeply and simply . . . be.

Through guiding others at Sedona Mago, I came to understand the vision Ilchi Lee had for this sacred land. It's not solely about the stunning scenery or the peace that pervades; it's about the deep inner transformation that unfolds when one fully connects with their true self. For me, Mago symbolizes the journey of self-discovery and the healing that comes from embracing one's essence. Ilchi Lee established this site to foster love for oneself and the Earth. He often shared with visitors that while Sedona's beauty is undeniable, the soul that perceives this beauty is even more magnificent.

Together with Ilchi Lee, I warmly invite you to Sedona Mago, in a heartfelt call to those seeking deeper self-connection and a genuine path to healing. If you're open to embracing the transformative work of self-discovery, the Love Heals Retreat at Mago is ready to welcome you.

This book aims to share the foundational concepts and practices integral to the Love Heals Retreat, yet the true essence of this experience can be most fully appreciated through being here. Surrounded by a supportive community with shared goals, you're invited to embark on a journey of healing and self-discovery that promises to be unlike any other. I look forward to the opportunity of welcoming you to Sedona Mago, where your journey toward healing and self-realization can begin anew.

Love Heals Together

My healing journey, alongside that of Ilchi Lee and countless others, has opened my eyes to a simple truth: our journey of self-discovery goes far beyond ourselves. It has the power to touch the lives of others as well. This is the essence of "Love Heals Together," a movement I invite you to join.

At its core, this movement is about sharing the love and healing we've experienced with those around us and beyond. It encourages simple acts, such as watching the *Love Heals* film with friends and family and sharing healing practices and personal stories.

In a world full of challenges and divisions, love is a force that can cross any boundary, bridge any gap, and spark positive change. Now more than ever, we need to amplify messages of love and unity to counteract separation and negativity, fostering compassion and understanding. Love can heal, bring joy, and unite us all, no matter where we come from.

The easiest way to be part of this movement is to share what you've learned about love and healing. Consider those facing similar challenges when you cultivate and send healing energy to yourself. Offer a moment of intention for their relief alongside yours.

Extend this compassion further to all life and the very soul of our planet. The power of love knows no limits.

Thank you deeply for allowing me to accompany you on your healing journey. I sincerely hope to meet you in person and continue to share this path of love and healing together.

Practice Index

Acknowledgments

We, Ilchi Lee and I, extend our deepest gratitude to everyone whose dedication, expertise, and support have been essential in bringing this book to life.

A special thank you to Bruce H. Lipton, PhD, Les Aria, PhD, Fred Luskin, PhD, David Hanscom, MD, and Yolessa Lawrinnce, for your generous sharing of your expert insight and wisdom, which has significantly enriched this work.

Our profound appreciation goes to the *Love Heals* film production team, including Krisanna Sexton, Dana Croschere, Sohyung Lim, and Ericka Crawford, PhD. Your dedication, creativity, and relentless effort have been vital in realizing this project.

Heartfelt thanks to Jiyoung Oh, Michela Mangia-racina, and Nicole Dean for your editorial expertise. Your unwavering support, meticulous attention to detail, and insightful feedback have been crucial in the development of this book.

To Kiryl Lysenka, whose beautiful design has elevated the presentation of this book.

Lastly, we offer our special thanks to the courageous individuals who shared their beautiful healing journeys with us. Your stories are the heart of this book, inspiring hope and healing in others.

Resources

Love Heals Film

The *Love Heals* film documents the journey of Dana and 18 others as they explore healing and self-discovery through ancient energy principles. Its official website is a resource for those interested in the film's backstory, viewing options, related retreats and workshops, and the Love Heals Together campaign. For more information, visit LoveHealsFilm.com.

Body & Brain Yoga Tai Chi Centers

Body & Brain Yoga Tai Chi centers offer classes in yoga, tai chi, and meditation based on Brain Education and energy principles. There are about 80 centers across the U.S. with more in South Korea, Japan, Europe, Canada, and New Zealand. Group classes, workshops, and individual sessions are available both in person and online. Find a U.S. center near you at BodynBrain.com.

Sedona Mago Center for Well-being and Retreat

Located among the red rocks of northern Arizona, Sedona Mago Center provides retreats and programs focused on personal development, health and wellness, and spirituality. Renowned for the restorative power of its breathtaking landscape, it serves as the exclusive venue for the Love Heals Retreat. For more information, visit SedonaMagoRetreat.org.

Brain Education TV

Brain Education TV is a YouTube channel dedicated to mental health and wellness resources. Its videos support individuals coping with stress, depression, and anxiety by offering practical insights and techniques. Explore exercise videos aligned with the energy principles discussed in this book at YouTube.com/@BrainEducationTV.

Love Heals Retreat

The Love Heals Retreat is a structured five-day program held in Sedona, AZ, which aims to facilitate personal growth and healing. This retreat, highlighted in the *Love Heals* film, focuses on connecting participants

LEARN MORE

with their true selves and enhancing the natural healing capabilities of the body, mind, and spirit. For more information, scan the QR code.

Books of Related Interest

The following books by Ilchi Lee can help you understand and deepen the energy practices introduced in this guide. See them all and more related books at BestLifeMedia.com.

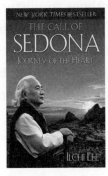

The Call of Sedona:
Journey of the Heart

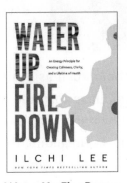

Water Up Fire Down:
An Energy Principle for
Creating Calmness, Clarity,
and a Lifetime of Health

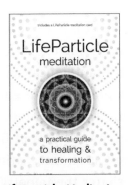

LifeParticle Meditation:
A Practical Guide to Healing
and Transformation

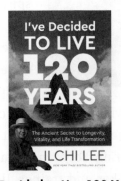

I've Decided to Live 120 Years:
The Ancient Secret
to Longevity, Vitality,
and Life Transformation

About the Authors

Ilchi Lee is a visionary, mentor, and educator who has devoted his life to teaching energy principles and developing methods to nurture the full potential of the human brain. He developed mind-body training methods such as Brain Education and Body & Brain, which have inspired many people worldwide to live healthier and happier lives. Lee has penned more than 40 books, including the *New York Times* bestseller, *The Call of Sedona: Journey of the Heart,* as well as *The Art of Coexistence: How You and I Can Save the World.* For more information about Ilchi Lee and his work, visit ilchi.com.

Ilchibuko Todd is an accomplished spiritual teacher, speaker, and artist. She brings more than 20 years of expertise in mastering energy principles through Brain Education and Body & Brain practice. She guides individuals to deeply connect with their true selves and unleash their greatest potential. As the CEO of Body & Brain Yoga and Health, as well as an international speaker and trainer, Ilchibuko shares the importance of self-healing as the foundational step toward healing humanity and the planet. For more information about Ilchibuko Todd and her work, visit ilchibuko.com.